The Bones of the Others

THE BONES OF THE OTHERS

The Hemingway Text
from the Lost Manuscripts
to the Posthumous Novels

HILARY K. JUSTICE

The Kent State University Press
KENT, OHIO

© 2006 by The Kent State University Press, Kent, Ohio 44242

ALL RIGHTS RESERVED

Library of Congress Catalog Card Number 2006011515

ISBN-13: 978-0-87338-875-7

ISBN-10: 0-87338-875-5

Manufactured in the United States of America

10 09 08 07 06   5 4 3 2 1

LIBRARY OF CONGRESS CATALOGING-IN-PUBLICATION DATA

Justice, Hilary K., 1966–

The bones of the others : the Hemingway text from the lost manuscripts to
the posthumous novels / Hilary K. Justice.

p.   cm.

Includes bibliographical references and index.

ISBN-13: 978-0-87338-875-7 (hardcover : alk. paper) ∞

ISBN-10: 0-87338-875-5 (hardcover : alk. paper) ∞

1. Hemingway, Ernest, 1899–1961—Criticism and interpretation.

2. Hemingway, Ernest, 1899–1961—Manuscripts.

I. Title.

PS3515.E37Z656 2006

813'.52—dc22   2006011515

British Library Cataloging-in-Publication data are available.

For Norma Seim and Jim Justice,
and in memory of Paul Smith

CONTENTS

ACKNOWLEDGMENTS

To express my gratitude to everyone who has made this work possible would take another book. Here are but a few of them.

My deepest gratitude to the following organizations and groups, who generously provided financial support for research and travel, without which this work would not have been possible:

The Andrew W. Mellon Foundation
The Humanities Division and the Department of English Language and Literature of the University of Chicago
The College of Arts and Sciences, Illinois State University
The Hemingway Foundation and Society
The John F. Kennedy Library Foundation
The Paul Smith Founders Fellowship Committee
The Ernest Hemingway Foundation of Oak Park
The family and friends of James Hinkle
The family and friends of Marcia Tillotson
My friends and family

Public thanks of a professional and personal nature are due the following people: of the University of Chicago: Bill Veeder, David Bevington, Bill Brown, Janice Knight, Bruce Redford, Colleen Boggs, Martha and Tim Bohrer, Rebecca Chung, and Patty and Scott Lewis; of Northeastern Illinois University: Donald Hoffman; of Trinity College: Paul Smith, Ron Thomas, Arthur Feinsod, Milla Riggio; of Dartmouth College: Bill Summers, Melinda O'Neal, Harry Ritchie, Jon Appleton, and Peter Travis.

I am profoundly indebted to Stephen Plotkin, Megan Desnoyers, and James Roth of the John F. Kennedy Library in Boston.

Thanks are also due to the intrepid scholars who keep Hemingway studies vital and endlessly fascinating. They are too numerous to name here, but a few, a happy few, deserve especial mention for their support of this project: the late Paul Smith, whose pointed arguments and bold laughter punctuated the birth of this idea; Susan Beegel, who provided generous encouragement at all stages; and Robert Trogdon, whose faith, patience, and photographic memory made completing this work a joy. Also, my thanks to Jim Meredith, Kirk Curnutt, Linda Patterson Miller, Carl Eby, Rose Marie Burwell, Jennifer Wheeler, Jackson Bryer, Miriam Mandel, Gerry Brenner, Jerry Kennedy, Ken Panda, Amy Vondrak, Tracy Banis, Jacque Brogan, the late Mike Reynolds, and Linda Wagner-Martin. The late Wes Tiffney will always hold a special place in my heart for keeping me so well entertained by e-mail.

A special thank you, for their hospitality and efforts on behalf of Hemingway in Cuba, to Gladys Rodriguez, Danilo Arrate, Frank and María Valdes at the Finca Vigía in San Francisco de Paula; Mario Masvidal at the Instituto Superior des Artes; Carmen Fournier, Modesta (Molly) Correoso, and especially the late Gregorio Fuentes, for saving the Pilar and for an unforgettable moment in Cojímar.

Special thanks to my colleagues at Illinois State University for their varied contributions to this project, especially Christopher Breu, Tim Hunt, Janice Neuleib, Jerry Savage, Rodger Tarr, Torri Thompson, and Roberta Trites.

I am especially grateful to all my students, especially Jeffrey Ludwig, Kevin McKinnon, Christopher Howard, Jonathan Myers, Melany Green, Jessi Lim, and Anthony McGinn, for their fine, creative thinking on Hemingway. Special thanks are due to Jeffrey Ludwig and April Chapman for their editing assistance.

I am, as always, indebted to those who know me as writer first and author second—they have suffered the most in the transition. Thanks to my mother, Norma Seim; my father, Jim Justice; and the rest of my family—Terry Justice, Mike Justice, Drew and Patsy Justice, Karl and Janie Seim, and Herbert and Sally Napier. Thanks are also due to Tom McDonough, David Kovar, Stephen Carter, Chris Robinson, Scott Benjamin, and Jesse Robbins.

No one has ever laughed as loudly through as much as *las Chicas:* Ann McDonough, Anne Brennan, Rebecca Kovar, Kelli Seaholm, Sherry Watt, and especially Rhonda Nicol (who did a brilliant job of midwifery on the final introduction).

My gratitude to Joanna Hildebrand Craig, Tara C. Lenington, and Christine Brooks, of the Kent State University Press. A special thanks to Michele Budden for her friendship and invaluable contributions to the preparation of the index.

A special kind of thanks to the young 'uns: Eliza, Morgan, Duncan, Jason, Jessica, Carrie, and Jake—all of whom provided distraction that I (sometimes) welcomed with enthusiasm—and to Billy, who can argue Harry Potter theory for hours. Also to the furballs: Riley, who kept my feet warm whilst I edited the final version, and Blake and Pseudo, who occasionally assisted, most creatively, with typing.

Finally, thanks are due to the Chicago Bulls (1996–1998), Julia Child, and J. K. Rowling for keeping me sane.

INTRODUCTION

THE HEMINGWAY TEXT

An author cannot of course remain wholly unaffected by his experience, but the ways in which a story-germ uses the soil of experience are extremely complex, and attempts to define the process are at best guesses from evidence that is inadequate and ambiguous.

    —J. R. R. Tolkien

J. R. R. Tolkien's assertion that in understanding a writer's creative process the best one can do is "guess" from evidence that is "inadequate and ambiguous" makes a kind of comfortable sense, and it is a wise reader and critic who heeds its implicit warning: "You can't know; don't bother to try; that way lies madness." Hemingway's published works seem to support Tolkien's sage advice. For decades, readers have found themselves curious but confounded in their desire for straightforward generic classifications. To cite only the latest example, Hemingway's most recently published full-length work, *True at First Light*, is subtitled *A Fictional Memoir*, yet the scholarly edition of the same work, *Under Kilimanjaro*, has been described as an autobiographical novel. Madness indeed. . . .

However, the implicit assumption in Tolkien's statement—that any investigation of "the ways in which a story-germ uses the soil of experience" has as its primary objective definition—is intrinsically proscriptive. Reading Ernest Hemingway's early works in light of the posthumously published novels, and vice versa, while granting equal privilege to published works and to archival material, allows readers and researchers alike to challenge assumptions such as Tolkien's regarding how much of a writer's creative process one may be able to understand.

The publication of Hemingway's posthumous works and the opening of related archival materials provide researchers with a better quality of evidence than that which Tolkien describes. This in turn may locate scholarly "guesses" regarding how Hemingway transformed experience in writing with much greater proximity to the Platonic ideal of accuracy than was dreamt of in Professor Tolkien's Cartesian philosophy.

The evidence in Hemingway's case differs in both quantity and kind from the usual sources of evidence for the reconstruction of a writer's creative process. The difference in quantity stems from Hemingway's pack-rat tendency to save seemingly every scrap of paper he ever touched—what Charles Baudelaire called "the horrors that make up the sanctuary of art" (xxx). Furthermore, his last wife, Mary, knew Jacqueline Kennedy socially, which made it possible for his papers to be preserved in the John F. Kennedy Library. Finally, a revolution froze many of his ephemeral assets, entombing them in a time capsule as the property of the people of Cuba and thus precluding their dispersal and probable disposal.

Access to the posthumous novels and their archival matrices provides evidence that also differs in kind, enabling readers to not only read individual texts but also perceive the fluidity of their intertextual relationships and investigate the lines of connection Hemingway himself drew between textual incidences of oft-recurring structures, images, and phrases. One can thus begin to identify the teleological fluidities in his work, something he analogized as "autobiography by *remate*," remate being the jai alai term for a pass that bounces off not one but two walls between players (quoted in Burwell 203n). Although he used the term in 1958 to describe what he was doing with his Paris sketches (published posthumously as *A Moveable Feast*), much if not all of his writing was composed thus: his present emotions evoked recent memories, which in turn evoked older ones, including memories of previously written stories. All these sources would emerge, transformed, in sets of apparently unrelated but intricately interwoven texts. These multidirectional, intertextual fluidities liberate scholars from the specific strictures of various critical schools and methodologies—textual and literary scholars need not work backward in order to reconstruct an evolutionary model, and psychoanalytic and cultural scholars are not obligated to construct an atemporal authorial persona that is impervious to change over time in order to pursue specific lines of inquiry.

By the time Hemingway was writing *The Garden of Eden,* he had come to understand his writing as a single, fluid text, despite his having published discrete, apparently unrelated portions of it under separate titles. His understanding of his creative process provides focus for inquiries into "the Hemingway Text," broadly defined by Nancy Comley and Robert Scholes as the entirety of his published oeuvre, archival material, and (for their purposes) "a cultural matrix that we share with Hemingway, as this matrix appears when we imagine Ernest Hemingway at the center of it" (x). Although Comley and Scholes put "the questions of gender ahead of all others" (ix), their general concept of the Text is amenable to other kinds of critical inquiry, especially textual investigations of creative process, writerly subjectivity, and the social construction of authorship.

Every Hemingway work challenges readers to consider his texts' relationships to each other. Although there are several excellent critical studies that consider evidence from the conjunction of multiple works, few scholars realize the potential radical redirection of textual inquiry made possible by access to the posthumously published material. Many critics use the early short story "The Sea Change" as a lens through which to read the late work *The Garden of Eden.* They note associative resonances between the two—the mirror behind the bar, the bisexuality of the protagonists—but none follow the implicit argument to its logical conclusion: that the early story may be considered a kind of microcosmic draft of the much later novel. Paul Smith, in a move nearly unique in Hemingway criticism, reverses the usual chronological direction of textual inquiry and proposes *The Garden of Eden* as the lens through which to read "The Sea Change." This approach lends credence to the conclusion that the protagonist of "The Sea Change" is, like his descendent in *Eden,* a writer and also supports Robert Fleming's argument that the story's psychosexual effect is complicated by the protagonist's compulsion to publish intimacies that for most people remain private. Smith stops shy of calling *Eden* a later draft of "The Sea Change," but, again, that would be the logical extension of his argument.

Smith's reversal of the usual teleology of textual inquiry is profoundly interesting for the possibilities it opens for a similar consideration of the Hemingway Text as a whole. Using manuscript evidence to investigate how the late and early works may specifically inform each other reveals a cycle of textual dialogics in which chronological linearity must finally be subordinated to Hemingway's own fluidity, wherein patterns resembling the fractals of mathematical chaos theory emerge. These patterns reveal much about the inadequacies of assumptions concerning the boundaries that published titles place around "individual" Hemingway works.

From a vantage point beyond those illusory boundaries, Hemingway's writing is revealed as a lifelong exploration of the public and the private. His works, collectively and individually, explore the productive tensions between paired concepts: fertility and virility, vocation and occupation, short fiction and novel, and writer and author. Each of these conceptual pairs reveals some nuance of issues surrounding publishing, or "making public." For Hemingway, the public-private boundary marked the salient difference between fertility and virility (fertility seems for him to have had a private nuance, and virility one of public performance) and between vocation and occupation (occupation being the public performance of vocation). More obviously, publication marks the professional boundary between writer and author. Viewing Hemingway's works retrospectively reveals a fluid overarching unity that provides a useful critical lens through which to examine finite moments and broader trends.

In the early 1920s, of course, Hemingway could not know that the permeability of the public-private boundary would occupy and preoccupy him throughout his life. Nor could he suspect that the ideas, locations, and even the very words of his early work would evolve and reappear, transformed, in much of his subsequent writing. He did, however, distinguish between two kinds of stories he planned to write, labeling them "Personal" and "Authentic." He appeared to assign these categories according to his distance from his subject and the roles he played in relation to it: Personal refers to things he had done and experienced, in which he had played an actively participatory role, Authentic to things he had heard or witnessed, in which his role was that of the journalist, the observer, the voyeur. These categories would broadly inform his writing throughout his life, evolving into ever more overt explorations of private, subjective experience and public, objective observation.

As a writer still hoping for publication, Hemingway could not yet appreciate how authorship was a public role and, in relation to the published texts on which it depends, a static one; nor could he predict that he would later question and complicate that role to which he still only aspired. He could not yet anticipate that, as a writer, his relationship to his works would remain fluid and that he would return to them decades later, when, as an author, celebrity, and icon, he would again wish for what he didn't have—to be only a writer, unencumbered by his public roles. And he could not yet have the perspective on his own creative process to articulate what in retrospect would become obvious: that in his Personal writing, he would always represent his emotional response to his current situation by refracting it through his past, finding emotional points of contiguity between his present and his past, and using this doubled emotional intensity to make his readers "feel more than they understand," the purpose of Hemingway's "theory of omission" (*Moveable Feast* 75).

In the early 1930s, in *Death in the Afternoon,* Hemingway offered his iceberg theory of writing: "If a writer of prose knows enough about what he is writing about he may omit things that he knows and the reader, if the writer is writing truly enough, will have a feeling of those things as strongly as though the writer had stated them. The dignity of movement of an iceberg [*sic*] is due to only one-eighth of it being above water" (192).

The seven-eighths of the story that remained submerged was not comprised of coyly withheld information about the events represented in the story, as many have understood the iceberg theory, in part because of Hemingway's assertion in *A Moveable Feast* that the thing omitted from "Out of Season" was Peduzzi's suicide, which the reader was somehow supposed to "feel" (75).[1] What was left out of the words, if not the writing, of his Personal fiction was its pertinence to his current situation. The Personal fiction was all immediately autobiographical but in a way that only his intimate circle—his wives and closest friends and, later, his children—could possibly understand. Only they would know what current situation prompted him to write a particular story at a particular time.

Hemingway's early stories appear to be full of gaps in which much of what happens is not represented explicitly in the text; it is tempting to locate the seven-eighths of the iceberg in those gaps. The characters' interiority—their emotions, their thoughts, and their impetus toward change—is rarely, if ever, explicit in his early fiction, thus prompting reader responses like "But nothing happens in this story. All he does is go fishing," or "All they do is have an argument, and then the maid comes in with a cat." These emotions, however, are the point of contiguity between why Hemingway wrote what he did when he did and what he actually wrote about. By implying his characters' emotional realities, he risked exposing his own response to his immediate situation.

This risk, which Hemingway located in the tension between the conceptual pairs (Personal/Authentic, public/private, fertility/virility, etc.) that overtly or implicitly informed his writing, provides a key to understanding his creative process. The reader's first challenge is to determine how the immediate context of writing is manifest in his texts; the second, to determine points of contiguity between immediate context and past events and, later, stories. The latter is the greater challenge, especially when examining his late works. Because the mature Hemingway's memories included the experience of writing earlier stories, memories of that writing would necessarily rekindle the complex emotional resonances from which these earlier stories arose.

When one considers Hemingway's works as they have appeared in print, it is nearly impossible to discern Hemingway's larger creative and writerly purpose and to understand his works within the context of this purpose. The order in which the short fiction was presented in collection (*In Our Time,* 1925; *Men Without Women,* 1927; and *Winner Take Nothing,* 1933) impedes contextual inquiry, and no collection since has privileged composition order. The posthumously published Personal works, *Islands in the Stream* and *The Garden of Eden* (and the less Personal *A Moveable Feast* and *True at First Light*), not only appeared out of composition order but were heavily and invisibly edited, finally "authored" by someone other than Hemingway. But composition order is crucial to understanding the Hemingway Text, because nearly everything he wrote was in some way autobiographical, and the more material one has to work with, the better. This is especially true of the Personal writing, in which the context of composition is often the single most important determinant of what a single work is about—and the least obvious.

Examining the dates of composition for Hemingway's early short fiction reveals a pattern of two twinned trajectories that are currently understood, separately, as the so-called marriage tales and selected Nick Adams stories. These labels are complicated slightly by the revelation that the stories—more accurately identified as "fertility tales" and "virility tales," respectively—do not end in the late 1920s and are not limited to his short fiction. They reappear, doubled, in the novels Hemingway began after World War II: *Islands in the Stream* and *The Garden of Eden.*

Recent larger psychosexual critical projects, such as Spilka's *Hemingway's Quarrel with Androgyny* and Eby's *Hemingway's Fetishism,* tend to focus primarily on *The Garden of Eden.* The reasons for this are perhaps obvious; *The Garden of Eden* is nothing if not a sensual novel, one in which cross-gendered, androgynous, and homosexual eroticism is central to the plot. The mental illness evinced by two of its female characters, only one of whom appears in the published version, renders it particularly rich for feminist and gender-based inquiry as well, as demonstrated by Comley and Scholes in *Hemingway's Genders: Rereading the Hemingway Text* and by Comley in "Madwomen on the Riviera." The novel invites readers and critics alike to revise or reconfirm their impressions of "Hemingway the manly man" based on the work's status as partially autobiographical. Although neither study references the Personal-Authentic list, they both focus primarily on works in the Personal category. Neither project addresses what this unfinished novel may reveal about Hemingway as a writer with a consistent and identifiable long-term project dating from his earliest work; this writer had a far different relationship to his writing and a far more sophisticated understanding of the ways in which publication complicates creativity, whether textual or sexual, than has yet been suspected or addressed.

As published, *The Garden of Eden* proposes a kind of later edition of many of Hemingway's own earlier Personal works. As it was written, however, it is also deeply indebted to the more Authentic *Death in the Afternoon,* with its overarching concerns with the necessarily destructive mechanisms whereby art is made public. The idea of the dangers of publication links all the novel's concerns, from androgynous haircuts to distinctions between literary genres to the tensions between identity and role: gender roles, sexual role-play, and the role of the writer/author.

Taken together, both of these works ask and answer a question that has lingered in the minds of reviewers, readers, and critics since the appearance of *Death in the Afternoon* in 1932: What happened to Hemingway in the 1930s? The answer may be found in the ways in which the strands of his writing began to entwine around the concept of publication.

None of the works published during that decade received anything like the positive critical reception his earlier work had generated. Between *A Farewell to Arms* (1929) and *For Whom the Bell Tolls* (1940), his new work—*Death in the Afternoon* (1932), *Winner Take Nothing* (a collection of short fiction, 1933), *Green Hills of Africa* (1935), *To Have and Have Not* (1937), and *The Fifth Column* (a play, which opened in 1940)—received mixed reviews at best. Literary critics ranging from historicists to Marxists argue that Hemingway was, by 1930, a dinosaur, out of step with the Great Depression and the socially minded 1930s. Other critics argue that during this decade Hemingway simply did not do his best work (other than a brief glimmer in 1936, with "The Snows of Kilimanjaro" and "A Short Happy Life of Francis Macomber").[2] Still others argue that the problems of fame were beginning to take their eventually tragic toll on Hemingway and his work (Raeburn). There is merit in all these positions, but the question of what happened to his writing in the 1930s may be refined and answered through the study of the contiguity between his early and late work. Something was different after *A Farewell to Arms,* certainly, and something got (momentarily) better with *For Whom the Bell Tolls,* but what, exactly, has yet to be explained from a textual perspective.

What was different was his understanding of the paradox of publication as a necessary danger for him as a writer and a dangerous necessity for him as an author. An understanding of *The Garden of Eden* in the larger context of his oeuvre reveals that between *A Farewell to Arms* in 1929 and the stories of the late 1930s, Hemingway consciously decided to abandon his Personal writing in favor of the Authentic. As the Personal writing disappeared, so did his practice of writing the fertility and virility narratives in pairs, so did the marriage tales, and, finally, so did Nick Adams. Coincidentally, Hemingway also largely abandoned fiction in favor of journalism and short fiction for longer forms.

Consideration of the Hemingway Text in its changing compositional contexts—in the context of other texts he was working on simultaneously, in addition to the obvious immediate and past biographical contexts—offers readers the opportunity to approach Hemingway's own understanding of his life's work. Combining elements of textual, biographical, and psychoanalytic inquiry produces a reconstruction of the writing moment, and this reconstruction facilitates a more complete understanding of a writer's creative process: a writer's relationship to his texts, the texts' relationship to the writer's present, and the texts' relationships to each other.

In this book, I trace the contextual evolution of three creative threads that make up one late work, *The Garden of Eden.* Two of these threads stem from Hemingway's earliest Personal short fiction and form something like a double helix comprised of the early so-called marriage tales and the Nick Adams stories that Hemingway paired with them, working on a pair of stories contemporaneously and thereby examining gendered aspects of a single thematic concern.

These Personal stories form a single strand in another kind of double helix, the other strand being what Hemingway called his Authentic works, which were more journalistic in tone, less concerned with heterosexual and homosocial relationships, more concerned with artistic questions examined in an objective tone that belies his implication in the systems under his scrutiny. The relative distance Hemingway perceived between himself and his subjects in these two categories is so problematic as to be nearly useless as a critical tool but not so as fictional object. Like all efforts predicated on paradox, Hemingway's efforts to erect and maintain boundaries between his personal and public lives, between his experience and his fiction, ultimately failed. But the permeability of those boundaries, and the boundaries that a single title inscribes around a work, constitutes the object in his late work *The Garden of Eden.*

To illustrate the problem of that permeability and its teleological fluidity within the Hemingway Text in greater specificity, and in plainer language, I offer a brief narrative skeleton, which will be fleshed out in the chapters that follow.

Just beyond the midway point of *True at First Light,* Hemingway pauses to invoke Dante in a backhanded aside designed to frustrate his wife Mary's artistic creativity. When she proposes writing a long poem about Africa, the Hemingway character/narrator counters that "Dante only made crazy people feel they could write good poetry." He then lets Dante drop until, in what would become chapter 16, the Hemingway character takes his solitary night walk, in which he encounters the three animals from the Book of Jeremiah (5:6): a wolf, a lion, and a leopard. These three animals figure prominently in William Faulkner's story "The Bear," which also alludes to the Book of Jeremiah and to the opening of Dante's *Inferno.* In *Inferno,* these animals achieve allegorical significance as the She-Wolf of Avarice—figured in Africa as the hyena, associated with the feminine scapegoat for artistic death in "The Snows of Kilimanjaro"; the lion of Ambition, figured here as Hemingway's latest sally against his rival Faulkner; and the spotted panther of Worldly Pleasure, figured in *True at First Light* as Mary Hemingway's Nairobi shopping trip. Hemingway's retroversion of details from the Bible, "The Bear," and *Inferno* does not bring him closer to the divine but rather discloses his reassessment of the terms of his contract with the secular—he finds them "expensive" (271), but because he has proven himself still capable of providing and appreciating material and physical pleasure, acceptable. "So far," he says, "it has been worth the price."

What price?

Keeping Dante in mind, one may find an answer to that question in *Death in the Afternoon,* in which, at the end of chapter 6, a "low dark passage" is opened at the sound of a trumpet by a man named Gabriel. Through these gates two characters enter the text: an Author and an Old Lady. Hemingway's *True at First Light* references to Dante and to Faulkner's story "The Bear," combined with Mary and Patrick Hemingway's separate assertions that Hemingway rarely traveled without his copy of *Inferno,* now allow for the speculation that Dante figures earlier and more centrally in his thinking than critics have considered. Reading *Death in the Afternoon* through the lens of Dante sheds light on the Author–Old Lady dialogues as a morality play on authorship—the business of publication—and its attendant dangers to the private craft of the writer, dangers that are figured specifically, if generically, as female.

The price Hemingway paid for the *True at First Light* safari was the exploitation of his celebrity to make it possible. While the Hemingway character embarks on his solitary night walk into the divine mysteries of the aging writer, Mary is shopping and having her hair done in Nairobi. Mary's creativity, like Catherine Bourne's, is limited to that of a small short-haired animal with which to achieve nocturnal ecstasy. In the daytime she becomes an exploitative parasite, endangering her husband's artistic vocation by requiring it to become a lucrative profession. Her role as muse is thus, like everything else in Africa, "true at first light" but "a lie by noon." And as soon as she suggests that she too might like to write, she is labeled "crazy"—a prophecy fulfilled for her in *The Garden of Eden* by the character of Catherine Bourne.

Catherine Bourne's desire to play "great publisher" to her writer/husband's already abandoned account of their honeymoon in *The Garden of Eden* begins to echo the deleterious effect the Old Lady has on the narrator and the character of the Author in *Death in the Afternoon.* Meanwhile, *The Garden of Eden*'s "other woman," Marita, functions as David's muse in a way that Catherine does not but very much wants to. Marita's function as such in *The Garden of Eden* thus cements the connections throughout the Hemingway Text between sexual and artistic creativity and fulfillment.

Reading "The Sea Change" through the lens of the posthumous *The Garden of Eden* raises the possibility that other early Hemingway stories figure rather centrally in moments of extreme tension in the later novel in a way that reciprocally illuminates similar moments in the earlier fiction. For instance, David and Catherine Bourne's first marital spat, in Madrid, variously echoes several of the early short stories: "Ten Indians," "Hills Like White Elephants" (David's lines), "Cat in the Rain" (Catherine's), "The Sea Change," and, obliquely, "Cross-Country Snow."

One section that was cut from the published version of *The Garden of Eden* repeats the associative path through the Personal fiction, outlined above, but depends on works in the Authentic category. The writer Andy, cut by the uncredited editor Tom Jenks, is, like David Bourne, another version of Ernest Hemingway. Dismissed by Mark Spilka as "square" because he has no interest in androgynous haircuts ("Barbershop" 360), Andy nonetheless emerges specifically as an echo of the Hemingway who wrote *Death in the Afternoon,* the book Hemingway's critics had least understood. Andy's description of his own book encapsulates the two final versions of the last chapter of *Death in the Afternoon*—the excised chapter 20 from the galley proofs and the chapter as published.

Finally, back to Catherine. Catherine dismisses Andy's writing—and Andy himself—as didactic. The fact that she has not read his book does not bother her, a characteristic she shares with many of *Death in the Afternoon*'s detractors. Echoing the limitations of the Old Lady, she flatly declares that you cannot learn to like things from a book. Catherine makes the assumptions Hemingway's critics had been making since *The Sun Also Rises,* the same assumptions David's critics make in the reviews his editors send him, the same assumptions that the Old Lady makes: that book and man are interchangeable and that the public representation of identity was an accurate reflection of identity. Despite all that has been written about Hemingway and the effects of celebrity on his art, his allowing such assumptions to continue was the price that the Hemingway of *True at First Light* finally decided had not been too high after all.

The challenge the Hemingway Text thus poses to readers and scholars is to hear all its parts simultaneously—to appreciate its intricacy as a kind of literary eight-voice fugue that ends with a gunshot. The challenge is not, finally, to our understanding of Hemingway, but to our own marriage to linear thinking as scholars, researchers, and readers. The body of Hemingway's work stops seeming a catalog of discrete, easily consumed pieces and instead is revealed as a lifelong project, both fictional memoir and autobiographical novel of excess.

The fractal-like patterns of the Hemingway Text necessarily render the ordering of the sections and chapters herein somewhat arbitrary. Because one's career as a writer necessarily initially predates the publication that denotes authorship, the first three chapters follow that professional chronology, beginning with a consideration of Hemingway's very early short fiction and ending with the composition of *The Garden of Eden.* The fourth chapter focuses specifically on a middle-period work, *Death in the Afternoon,* and more specifically on the metacritical inquiry into authorship he embedded within the Author–Old Lady dialogues. The fifth returns to his preprofessional years in Paris. But such organization is for convenience only; the only accurate representation of the Hemingway Text as he conceived, wrote, and understood it would be hypertextual. When describing a fractal system, a starting point is arbitrary; one must, however, start somewhere.

The first three chapters focus primarily on Hemingway's Personal writing and reveal that a writerly text may differ strongly from an authorial text (although they are linguistically identical) and that a writer's relationship to text does not necessarily change at the boundary of publication (the point at which he becomes, additionally, its author) he may revisit this text at other points in his career. Hemingway's revisitation of his texts reveals much about both early and later versions, even if they are conceived years apart.

"The Personal Stories I (Paris, 1923–1925)" traces Hemingway's early creative process, before his understanding of the writer-author difference began to emerge in his writing, and establishes the baseline to which he would try to return in the writing of *The Garden of Eden,* twenty-five years later. This chapter considers the early short fiction within its compositional contexts, and thus in order of composition, and establishes that during this period Hemingway worked his so-called Personal stories (the marriage tales and selected Nick Adams stories) in pairs. This compositional pairing is obscured by publication order, but understanding this pairing is necessary for two reasons: to understand individual stories, and to perceive his larger Personal and writerly projects in the years before he could count on publication: to master his craft, to achieve publication, and to explore and enact dually gendered aspects of his immediate, intimate, domestic situations.

"The Personal Stories II (Paris and Provence, 1926–1927)" traces the beginnings of the schism in Hemingway's professional subjectivity and locates the earliest cracking within the writing of slightly later, but still intertwined, marriage tales and Nick Adams stories. This chapter notes the beginnings of a shift in his writerly project as his professional status began to change (from hoping for publication to assuming it). These later stories, especially their drafts, reveal that Hemingway was beginning to manipulate his texts to capitalize on his new professional role, but still, at this time, toward purely personal ends. This chapter also positions two of the least understood marriage tales—"A Canary for One" and "Hills Like White Elephants," and by association their paired Nick Adams stories, "In Another Country" and "Now I Lay Me" (originally "In Another Country II") and "Ten Indians"—as touchstones to which Hemingway would later return, suggesting that these stories represented for him the high point of his early creative career, the point at which he had mastered his craft.

Understanding these texts as the writer did at their time of composition (rather than retrospectively or as isolated texts within larger collections) corrects critical misinterpretations of "Hills Like White Elephants" and "A Canary for One." Within their compositional contexts, these stories may be understood as narrative palimpsests. They were written to achieve multiple objectives; both stories support dual, simultaneous, and mutually exclusive interpretations—one writerly, one authorial.

"The Necessary Danger: Writing *The Garden of Eden*" identifies this posthumous novel as Hemingway's textual autobiography, his fictional representation of his early creative process (specifically, the writing of the last of the paired stories discussed in the previous chapter, which were written in the time and place of *The Garden of Eden*'s setting). After situating the novel in its biographical context, this chapter delineates specific intertextualities among *The Garden of Eden,* these early stories, and—strangely—*Death in the*

Afternoon. The references to these earlier works are so overt that *The Garden of Eden* may be considered a later, highly evolved draft of them all. Although *The Garden of Eden* has contributed much to recent work on Hemingway and gender, androgyny, and fetishism, for Hemingway, these issues comprised but one side of a double helix similar to that in his earlier writing, the other side of which concerned writing, authorship, professionalism, and genre. What connects these two strands is the question of publication—of the boundary at which private roles (whether artistic or sexual) undergo a sea change, and at which perceptions alter irrevocably.

"A Pilgrim's Progress into Hell: *Death in the Afternoon* and the Problem of Authorship" locates Hemingway's metacritical project, his theoretical intervention, in the book's Author–Old Lady dialogues. Understood in this light, these dialogues reveal that, to Hemingway, his identity as a writer was relatively more important than his role as author, the role of author being the Hemingway on whom public and critical attention had been fixed since *A Farewell to Arms,* and the perception of which he had mocked in *Death in the Afternoon:* a dialogic social and legal construct, and therefore not real.

In the Author–Old Lady dialogues in *Death in the Afternoon,* the Author is as much a character as the Old Lady, and thus the Author in the book is not the author of the book. Three factors suggest that Hemingway constructed the Author character to criticize the critics (then reviewers): the generic distinction of the Author–Old Lady dialogues in the text, the timing of the composition of these dialogues within the context of correspondence Hemingway received from editors, and the book's initial critical reception. By waving the red cape of authorship at the critics, Hemingway was able to distract them from their legitimate business of addressing his works and thus to undercut the validity of their criticism when they instead attacked or applauded his personality—contemporary reviewers universally misidentified the Author character as Ernest Hemingway. *Death in the Afternoon,* understood in this light, presents Hemingway's overt realization and first textual representation of the schism between his writerly identity and authorial role, and of their relative value to him as a writer, if not as a man.

"Hemingway's Lost Manuscripts" reconstructs Hemingway's creative process within biographical, creative, and professional contexts, revealing that in the 1930s he began to focus on his Authentic writing, returning only intermittently to the Personal writing that had brought him early success. After World War II, however, he returned to the Personal writing in ways that both echoed and expanded upon his earlier work. For Hemingway, all the publication issues at play in his Personal writing (creation and transformation, intimacy and exposure, and fertility and virility) and in his Authentic writing (writer and author) centered finally on the issue of genre. He came to believe that his best artistic experiences were writing short fiction; he came to a sophisticated understanding of his creative process; and he would also come to understand that his process had evolved and demanded so much of him that he would never again achieve the perfect control of form that had distinguished him among other aspiring writers in expatriate Paris.

Paris was where he consciously reconstructed his creative process after the loss of his manuscripts in 1922. His first story written after that loss, "Out of Season," is a cross-gendered rewriting of one of the few stories that survived the loss, "Up in Michigan." Because of his lifelong creative process of regendering and revision, and because of the extent to which he gendered questions of private and public creation and transformation, of writing and authorship, he could no more give up the lost stories than could a mother stop seeking a lost child. I conclude, therefore, that the earliest Nick Adams stories were, in all probability, Hemingway's own revisions of the stories that were "lost" in 1922.

For those readers interested in the theoretical debates surrounding the problems of authorship and textuality, as well as a situation of this project's intervention therein, I include that discussion as the appendix.

CHAPTER ONE

THE PERSONAL STORIES I

(Paris, 1923–1925)

. . . if you are a genius and unsuccessful, everybody treats you as
if you were a genius . . .
—Gertude Stein, *Picasso*

In writing *The Garden of Eden,* the aging Hemingway attempted to redis-
cover and perhaps re-experience the writer he had been in the late 1920s, just
before the role of author began to dominate both his writing and his life.
Although the 1926 novel *The Sun Also Rises* had met with a certain success in
the United States, Hemingway was still living in Paris when it was published
and, as he would come to realize retrospectively, was enjoying his last years of
living in relative anonymity. Although he had been functioning in the more
socially implicated authorial role since the first of his works began to circu-
late publicly, and although his reputation was growing in the United States,
he was for the last time in his life among people who knew him as a person
first, a writer second, and as an author last. After his final years as a Paris
expatriate (1926–1928, permanently ending in 1930),[1] his reputation would
precede him; he would be a known (or at least recognized) quantity to nearly
everyone he met afterward.

In the late 1920s, however, Hemingway was less concerned with the demands
of his nascent public existence than with problems in his domestic life. In 1926,
he separated from his first wife, Hadley (who retained custody of their only
child, John), and awaited both the finalization of their divorce and a response
to his marriage proposal to his lover, Pauline Pfeiffer. In 1927, he and Pauline
were married, and in 1928, they had their first child. Although they maintained
their apartment in Paris, by 1929 they had decided to return to the United

States to settle in Key West. The year 1929 also brought with it two events that would permanently alter Hemingway's self-perception and his public status: his father's suicide, which left him the patriarch of a large extended family, many of whom (including his mother) would rely on him financially, and the publication of *A Farewell to Arms,* the novel that publicly cemented his critical reputation and sealed his public identity as a famous author.

Between 1923 and 1927, Hemingway wrote many of what he considered his best short narratives. For the first time in his life, his craft was equal to his talent; for the last, his fame was not yet equal to either. This was a honeymoon period, the period of the writer, the period to which an increasingly Proustian Hemingway[2] would attempt later to return by writing what would become *The Garden of Eden,* one of several *temps retrouvé* works left unfinished at his death, and the one that references these earliest writings, especially the early honeymoon fiction.

The early honeymoon fiction, "Hills Like White Elephants" and "Ten Indians," marks the end points of two series of stories, which, taken together, form a kind of double helix in Hemingway's early writing: the marriage tales and the Nick Adams stories (see table 1). Prior to the writing of "Cross-Country Snow," Hemingway used the writing of these series, in pairs, as a doubled project that allowed him to objectify and analyze gendered relationships while also escaping, partially, from the pressures of needing to do so. In writing *The Garden of Eden,* Hemingway relied very heavily on the composition, themes, and images of the endpoint stories in these series and, to a lesser degree, on those written slightly earlier and slightly later. These series, taken together, present four major psychological issues with which Hemingway would struggle and on which he would rely to vitalize his writing: (1) problems in (and, after 1926, guilt over) heterosexual relationships, (2) escaping into the wilderness, (3) intergenerational homosocial betrayal, and (4) gender switching. These themes are addressed by the early stories as follows:

	Marriage Tales	*Nick Adams Stories*
The Early Fiction		
(1923–1924)	"Out of Season" (1)	"The End of Something" (1)
	"Cat in the Rain" (1)	"The Three-Day Blow" (1), (2), (3)
	"Cross-Country Snow" (1), (2), (3)	"The Doctor and the Doctor's Wife" (1), (2)
The Dark Period		
(Fall 1926)	"A Canary for One" (1)	"Now I Lay Me" (2), (3)

Marriage Tales	Nick Adams Stories
The Early Honeymoon	
Fiction (May 1927)	"Hills Like White Elephants" (1), (2), (4)	"Ten Indians" (1), (2), (3)

Hemingway's later reliance on these early stories, and their relationships to each other, assumes many guises, ranging far beyond the questions of gender and psychosexuality on which much of the critical response to *The Garden of Eden* and the Hemingway Text has focused.[3] The relationships between *The Garden of Eden* and these earlier texts certainly involve gender but often in the service of other issues, including the relationships between writerly and authorial roles. The most important aspect of these relationships is the way in which Hemingway maps his anxieties about the conflicting roles as writer and author onto questions of gender roles in their public and private representations. Related questions regarding the writerly processes of creation and transformation (and the relative value Hemingway later assigned to these processes) will also figure prominently in my discussion of his growing realization that these early psycho-social and -sexual issues were related to, and eventually became subordinate to, questions of writing and authorship.

The early honeymoon fiction (and its related serial predecessors) contributes sometimes microcosmically to the later novel, *The Garden of Eden.* Early, apparently unrelated compositional details from the early works evolve throughout Hemingway's career and Text, eventually forming a mosaic of the larger works and of larger patterns in Hemingway's career and Text. Table 1 (p. 20) provides a visual map that may be of some assistance in negotiating the details, allusions, themes, and images that, as *The Garden of Eden* shows, connect these early stories in hitherto unexplored ways.

In order to begin to account for the long-term development of writerly and authorial issues as they figure both in the Hemingway Text and in Hemingway's creative process, I use this chapter to examine the earliest published individual Hemingway works, which re-emerge, only slightly transformed, in *The Garden of Eden,* and the biographical moments relevant to their creation: those that the works address and, more importantly, those during which they were written. These works—and the writing of them—contain the textual origins of the preoccupations to which Hemingway would return later in his writing life. This chapter considers the autobiographical nature of these early works but from a slightly atypical angle. Rather than focusing exclusively on the autobiographical objects of these stories, I privilege their composition as being in itself an important autobiographical element, and one that often determines the more obviously autobiographical subject matter. When we try to understand Hemingway's stories, knowing which stories were written when (and considering why) is often more important than identifying their autobiographical objects. His choice of these early compositional moments as the past to which he strove to return in his later narratives thus reveals a metanarrative—the autobiography of the writer writing—that informs not only his later projects but also the entire (and almost entirely self-reflexive) Hemingway Text.

One of the central questions that emerges from the Hemingway Text concerns anxiety. Anxiety is obviously central to the production of *The Garden of Eden,* but limiting consideration to anxieties that involve gender and sexuality obscures a much larger, more subtly nuanced picture. The function of memory in Hemingway's transformation of earlier texts into *The Garden of Eden* provides a bridge from which he and his readers may observe and judge how earlier experiences and their writing transformed Hemingway, in his multiple roles as self, lover, husband, ex-husband, father, patriarch, and, perhaps most importantly, writer (but not, significantly, author—that role is conspicuous by its implied absence here; it is overtly addressed in other works). Each of the earlier Hemingway texts that resurfaces, however briefly, in The *Garden of Eden* is concerned with one or more of these multiple roles and with the problems stemming from managing them in private and in public.

The works under consideration identify a gap between 1924 and 1926; during that gap Hemingway's roles expanded dramatically. Initially he was husband and writer; between 1924 and 1926, he also became a father, an adulterous lover, and an author published for the first time in his native country.[4] This chapter focuses on the works written prior to that gap, the works of the early period, and addresses the relationship of the writer to those texts in their compositional contexts.

The Early Stories (1923–1924)

In his consideration of *The Garden of Eden* manuscript, Mark Spilka notes that Hemingway's writings "oscillate between novels of failed sexual relations (*The Sun Also Rises, A Farewell to Arms*) and tales of stoic male endurance" ("Barbershop" 367). At first glance, Spilka's categories may seem to map neatly onto Hemingway's early works—the marriage tales ("Out of Season," "Cat in the Rain," "Cross-Country Snow," "A Canary for One," and "Hills Like White Elephants" [Smith, *Guide* 207])[5] and the Nick Adams stories. On closer examination, however, certain Nick Adams stories reveal the opposite of male stoicism—these are the Personal Nick Adams stories that were written in pairs with the marriage tales, rather than the Authentic ones.[6] These paired Personal stories reveal neither stoicism nor failed sexual relations but rather combine to portray various aspects of dysfunctional—but not entirely malfunctional—gendered relationships. One of these Nick Adams stories, "Cross-Country Snow," is also a marriage tale.

Spilka also notes that during his 1927 Provence honeymoon with Pauline Pfeiffer, Hemingway completed "Hills Like White Elephants" and "Ten Indians," and he implies that the writing of these two stories represents another such oscillation (366). Although Hemingway's early compositions do seem to alternate between the marriage tales and the Nick Adams stories, if one admits prewriting as part of the composition process, then the composition of these kinds of stories does not so much oscillate as occur simultaneously.

In *Hemingway: The Postwar Years and the Posthumous Novels,* Rose Marie Burwell forwards the thesis that toward the end of his life, Hemingway's writing comprised a more or less unified "Ur-Text," and that each of the posthumous works constituted merely one portion of this Ur-Text. Hemingway's tendency to compose multiple related works simultaneously was also an important factor even in his earliest endeavors. And in writing the later works, he connected them not only with each other but with the writing of the earlier works. Hemingway's personal view of writing thus encompasses and transcends the Ur-Text. In *The Garden of Eden,* he illustrates that time spent writing intimates the timelessness and placelessness that Mircea Eliade defines as "the Sacred," a space to which he eventually had to struggle to return. Focusing *The Garden of Eden* on the compositional context of the Personal fiction from the 1920s seems to have catalyzed that return.

After the very early "Out of Season," the composition date for each of the marriage tales corresponds to that of a seemingly unrelated Nick Adams story (see table 1). The composition dates of these stories indicate that, for Hemingway, the marriage tales were not separate from but, rather, somehow entwined with these specific Nick Adams stories, most of which concern Nick's childhood in Michigan.

Taken together, these two sequences highlight two initially disparate but increasingly related kinds of problems and anxieties as they first appear in the Hemingway Text, the first being writerly problems arising from conflict in and among his multiple private roles—how to find the time and space to write—and the second, authorial anxieties stemming from two mutually exclusive compulsions: to maintain personal and domestic privacy while transforming personal experience into published text.[7]

Table 1. Composition Dates

Marriage Tale	Composition Dates	Nick Adams Story	Composition Dates
"Cat in the Rain"	February / March 1924 (completed)**	"The End of Something" / "The Three-Day Blow"***	February / March 1924**
"Cross-Country Snow"*	April 1924	"The Doctor and the Doctor's Wife"	April 1924 (completed)
"A Canary for One"	September 1926 (completed)	"In Another Country" / "Now I Lay Me"***	September–December 1926
"Hills Like White Elephants"	May 1927	"Ten Indians"	May 1927 (completed)

*"Cross-Country Snow" is the only marriage tale in which Nick Adams appears.
**Reynolds places the composition dates for "Cat" and "The End" in February; Smith in March.
***"The Three-Day Blow" is a continuation of "The End of Something": "Now I Lay Me" was originally titled "In Another Country—Two" (KL/EH 120b and 120c.

The winter of 1922 changed Hemingway's life as a writer and as a man; in 1923, he addressed these changes, obliquely, in "Out of Season," the first of the marriage tales. In 1922, Hemingway lost nearly all his writing to that date. When preparing to leave Paris to join her husband on a skiing trip, Hadley packed Hemingway's drafts and carbons into a valise, which was then stolen at the Gare du Lyon. Only a few months later, Hadley would announce that she was pregnant, and Hemingway would famously inform Gertrude Stein that he was too young to be a father (Stein 262; see also Johnston 262; Smith, *Guide* 19).

Although neither fatherhood nor the loss of the manuscripts appears directly in the text of "Out of Season," this was the first published story he wrote after absorbing the impact of these Personal and writerly changes. Originally titled "Before the Season" (KL/EH 644, 1), the story depicts an argument between a married couple concerning, at least on the surface, fishing before the start of the legal season. That the argument has its roots in something else is obvious; what that something else might be is as obscure to the reader as it seems to be to the characters—and as such is beside the point of the story. Any resolution to the argument must wait, just as the fishing must wait: Peduzzi, the fishing guide, has forgotten the *piombo* (the lead sinker), without which the fishhook cannot pierce the surface of the water. The arguing couple likewise cannot, without something equally necessary (and similarly absent), pierce the surface of what is obviously a much deeper problem. It is too early for fishing, and too early for the couple to resolve their problems, whatever they may be.[8]

At the time of the story's composition, Hemingway clearly considered 1923 too early for him to be a father. Given his conservative (not to say Victorian) Oak Park, Illinois, upbringing and the poverty he later exaggerated when revisiting the Paris years (during which he claimed to have killed pigeons for food in the Luxembourg Gardens [Hotchner 45; *Islands* 60]), one might assume that his reluctance to embrace fatherhood stemmed from financial concerns. But in 1923 the connection between his domestic and professional economies was not entirely fiscal. Hemingway was not yet supporting himself with his fiction writing; he was still working as a journalist and relying on Hadley's trust fund. However, his image of himself as an emerging voice in modernism did not mesh with the responsibilities of providing for a family.[9] Hemingway was probably more worried about the changes fatherhood would work on his writing than about the strain on their finances. He had found in Europe the freedom to pursue the experience necessary to him as a man and as a writer. That experience to him meant travel, and a child meant encumbrance—thus the probable origin of the suitcase as a doubled metaphor for both fatherhood and writing, a metaphor that would figure centrally in both "Hills Like White Elephants" and *The Garden of Eden*.

After "Out of Season," each marriage tale was paired with a Nick Adams story as Hemingway negotiated the increasing discrepancy and conflict between two sets of responsibilities: to himself and his writing, and to Hadley and their son John, who was born in Toronto in October 1923. In writing the marriage tales, he explored various facets of the breakdown of his marriage to Hadley; in writing the Nick Adams tales, he apparently sought the restorative of the Michigan woods, which had provided him the site of his greatest childhood and adolescent freedom. Yet even the woods, and especially the writing of them, could not provide a complete escape. Each of these Nick Adams stories is concerned with the paradox of romantic relationships. Whether in the act of writing or within the text itself, the urge to escape gendered relationships is as strong as the urge to stay or, having left, to return. The marriage tales isolate tensions in a relationship; in the Nick Adams stories, Hemingway privileges the effects of relationship tensions on one individual.

The knowledge that these stories were written together in pairs reveals a more complete project in the writer's mind than does approaching each story individually. In the Nick Adams stories, his sympathy lies primarily with Nick; in the marriage tales, his greater sympathy is for the female characters.[10] Taken together, they represent the writer's attempt to see both sides of gendered re-lationships. Further, the compositional pairing of the stories reveals that the young Hemingway was trying for a much more subtly nuanced and sympa-thetic understanding of heterosexual relationships than critics of his later im-age as a macho misogynist prefer to believe.

When the Hemingways returned to Paris in January 1924, Ernest aban-doned journalism to focus exclusively on fiction writing despite the added expense of having a child. The first stories he completed after their return were "Cat in the Rain" and "The End of Something" (followed by its sequel, "The Three-Day Blow"). The marriage tale "Cat in the Rain" was set in Rap-pallo, Italy, where Ernest and Hadley had visited Ezra Pound the year be-fore, and where Hemingway had written "Out of Season." Although the exact date Hadley told Ernest about her pregnancy is unknown, she must have discovered it during the Italy trip—certainly by their March visit to Cortina, the setting for "Out of Season," and perhaps as early as Rappallo (Reynolds, *Chronology* 30–31; Smith, *Guide* 44).

"Cat in the Rain," like "Out of Season," takes as its subject the nameless underlying tensions that divide a husband and wife. Again, the exact cause of the tensions is unstated. The story, claustrophobically set in a hotel room on a monotonous, rainy day, portrays a wife who evinces her boredom by listing her wants. This list begins with a cat she sees through the window, continues with a litany of images seemingly designed deliberately to evoke the domes-tic stability of the previous generation—indicated in part by a wish to wear her hair long, in a bun, rather than in a 1920s boyish bob—and ends where it started, petulantly, with "I want a cat. I want a cat now. If I can't have long hair or any fun, I can have a cat" (131).

Critics have seized on the wife's desire for a cat as symbolic of her true desire for a baby (see Hagopian 221; White 243; Smith, *Guide* 46–48), and on this desire as the key to the entire story. Whether or not this is the case—and Hemingway leaves that deliberately ambiguous—is not the point. Although her restlessness and irritability (with the weather, the impermanence of their hotel room, and finally her husband George) may suggest the influence of hormones, her seizing on seemingly trivial, external matters and her unsuc-cessful attempt to address an unidentified deeper problem is central to the story. Whether or not "Cat in the Rain," considered alone, and innocent of biographical associations, must lead directly to the conclusion that the wife wants a baby (and excised portions of the "Cross-Country Snow" manuscript suggest that that may be exactly what Hemingway was thinking, as I will discuss later), it does provide, in very few pages, a concise, meticulous survey of a moment in a marriage when things have gone at least slightly wrong. If the couple's inability to communicate is any indication, these indeterminate, unsubstantial things will likely get worse. Had Hemingway's characters attempted to document "irreconcilable differences" before a divorce tribunal, "Cat in the Rain" and "Out of Season" certainly could have stood as illustrative examples of such differences, however difficult to name.

Their very insubstantiality, or un-name-ability, may in fact be the problem,[11] in a manner that anticipates Betty Friedan's identification of "the problem that has no name,"[12] a problem that registers, on the surface, as petulance and boredom. Hemingway addresses this problem from a different angle in the Nick Adams stories that he wrote concurrently with "Cat in the Rain." In "The End of Something" and its immediate sequel, "The Three-Day Blow," the problem gets a name, demonstrably the wrong one, in a line that has come to be attributed to Hemingway as man, not writer. In "The Three-Day Blow," Bill, a slightly older character to whom the younger Nick Adams has turned for relationship advice, asserts that "Once a man is married he's absolutely bitched" (90). Nick, Hemingway's alter ego in these stories, responds with silence, his usual response when he disagrees but does not, for whatever reason, want to argue.

In "The End of Something," Nick (apparently acting on Bill's earlier advice) ends his relationship with Marjorie; in "The Three-Day Blow," Nick regrets his decision. According to Bill's logic, the relationship would lead to marriage, and marriage is bad; therefore ending the relationship was the right choice; and, further, Marjorie's mother is undesirable—therefore Marjorie will be too, someday. But for Nick, Bill's logic is spurious. Nick is probably too young to consider marriage seriously (he is young enough, at least, that Bill must remind him to wear socks [86]). Bill's reasoning glances off the surface of Nick's feelings, which find not expression but only anesthesia in Bill's company, in their drinking, and in their heading into the woods to feel the storm of the title. The narrator, speaking from Nick's perspective, states that "Outside now the Marge business was no longer so tragic. It was not even very important. The wind blew everything like that away" (92). But the wind is ineffective; Nick, although drunk, thinks again that "None of it was important now. The wind blew it out of his head. Still he could always go into town Saturday night [NB: when Marge might be there]. It was a good thing to have in reserve" (93). Not even lighting out for the Michigan woods in the company of a good male friend, whether lived as experience or experienced while writing, provides adequate palliative for the Hemingway heart. By the end of the story, Hemingway has, with Nick's private thoughts, introduced the possibility that there may be more to marriage than being "bitched."

Nick's sympathies in this story are not with Bill and are not even entirely for himself. Nor are they for Marjorie, the girlfriend he left in "The End of Something." They are, however, for their relationship as it was before (i.e., before he took Bill's advice and ended what was, in its portrayal, a fun, relaxed, and happy companionship). There are too many aspects to relationships, and too many sides to the end of one, for Hemingway, even in his earliest writings, to propose one-sided judgments regarding them. Indeed, although his treatment of his wives may not have been entirely sympathetic, neither was it entirely selfish (especially in the early years of each marriage). When his stories are not considered through the distorting distraction of his later personal reputation, the subtle (albeit sometimes oblique) accuracy with which he presents the woman's side in his short fiction destabilizes accusations of misogyny that have bled over from accounts of Hemingway's personal life.[13] Although the responsibility for "the end of something" lies with Nick, Bill is the misogynist; Nick, confused and impressionable, has merely followed bad advice. He must weather the blows of the ensuing storm in the company of, but not in sympathy with, a friend whom he has learned not to trust.

In these four early stories, Hemingway has touched on and begun to explore not only the difficulty of naming one's intimate thoughts and feelings, but, with "The Three-Day Blow," the possible danger of making them public. The publication of what might best be left private was a central problem for Hemingway, both as a man and as a writer whose compulsion was to transform his lived and witnessed experience into publishable prose. In several instances, most notably regarding "Hills Like White Elephants," Hemingway would lie even when not pressed regarding the sources of his ideas. In an attempt to distance his private life from his writing, at least in interviews, he would claim that certain ideas, e.g., the abortion debate in "Hills," originated in overheard conversations rather than admit to their autobiographical sources. He would thus imply that his creative process relied on a combination of journalistic authenticity and writerly creativity rather than personal experience and writerly transformation.

In the next pair of stories, "The Doctor and the Doctor's Wife" and "Cross-Country Snow," written in the spring of 1924 (almost immediately after the previous pair), Hemingway temporarily abandoned the nameless problems (of the marriage tales) and the problem of the dangers lurking at the public-private boundary (of the previous Nick Adams story) to explore the problems of self-denial and intergenerational responsibility in families. (All these themes would reappear in the early honeymoon fiction, three years later.) In "Cross-Country Snow," the only one of the marriage tales in which Nick Adams appears, Nick is indulging in a final skiing trip before he and his wife move to the United States for the birth of their first child. In "The Doctor and the Doctor's Wife," Hemingway illustrates an episode in the dysfunctional marriage of Nick's parents, in which a very young Nick casts his sympathies and allegiance with his father, who appears to bear the emotional and psychological brunt in the marriage.

In these two stories, the marriage tale and Nick Adams sequences intersect. Both propose the limits of homosocial bonding, of "lighting out for the territory," as an alternative to the problems of romantic relationships; taken together in their composition, they place Nick in mirror image to himself, as child and as a soon-to-be father (in a later story, "Fathers and Sons," readers learn that Nick's own child is a boy). He is, however, ambivalent about both roles, and, at least in "The Doctor and the Doctor's Wife," these roles become confused as young Nick adopts the supportive role of manly companion to his emotionally and psychologically troubled father.

How much Nick, a child in "The Doctor and the Doctor's Wife," knows about the episode that establishes the father's character for the reader is unclear. In the story, Dr. Adams has hired several Native American men to saw logs that have escaped the logging company's flotilla and washed up on the beach in front of his Michigan cabin. The Native American men accuse him, rightly, of stealing. Angered and discouraged, Dr. Adams returns to the cabin where his wife—whom we learn is a Christian Scientist (75) and probably a hypochondriac—insidiously needles him from her bed in her (separate) bedroom, where she is nursing a headache (and, one may infer, a host of ills attendant on being the hypochondriacal Christian Scientist wife of a physician). Dr. Adams sits in his own room and cleans his shotgun[14] then leaves the cabin, only to be told by his wife "If you see Nick, dear, will you tell him his mother wants to see him?" (75)

Nick appears for the first time at the end of the story. His father finds him reading.

> "Your mother wants you to come and see her," the doctor said.
> "I want to go with you," Nick said.
> His father looked down at him.
> "All right. Come on, then," his father said. "Give me the book, I'll put it in my pocket."

"I know where there's black squirrels, Daddy," Nick said.

"All right," said his father. "Let's go there." (76)

The impact of Mrs. Adams's passive aggression on her family is under-scored in this story's ending. "If you see Nick . . . will you tell him" takes on the tone (if not the words) of command. Nick, who here provides the healthy end of the spectrum, linguistically asserts the strength of his own identity, countering "Your mother" with "I," "wants" with "want," "come" with "go," and "her [his mother]" with "you [his father]." Nick, already a better man than his father, offers him the solace of a naturalist's sojourn in the wilderness in search of the then-rare (and thus, to a boy, exciting) black squirrel. Even as a child, Nick instinctively realizes the potential escape in lighting out for the territory, and that the quest for an exciting trophy (or sighting) is in part only an excuse to go; already, he knows that such respite is and can only be temporary.

"Cross-Country Snow," the marriage tale in this pair, portrays another such temporary lighting out, but one with a definite and inarguably necessary terminus. In this story, Nick (in first drafts, Mike Adams) and his friend George go on what may be their final European skiing trip before both must return to the States—Nick for the birth of his child, and George to attend college. The text, as published, reveals little other than Nick's submission to the inevitable curtailment of freedom that fatherhood will impose on his lifestyle. An excised portion of the first draft, however, provides evidence in writing for the link between cats and babies that critics have argued for in the case of "Cat in the Rain."[15] In the excised pages of the draft, images of pregnancy abound, not the least of which is the pregnant waitress, here referred to as "the girl": "and drank the wine. It was in a big, /full-bellied/ heavy bottomed bottle. George poured the last of it evenly between Mike's [NB: later, Nick's] glass and his own. The girl /was singing/ came into the room and picked up a cat that had slipped through when she brought in the wine and went out. Let's have another bottle, Mike said" (KL/EH 345, 6; /deletions/).

Hemingway made several changes between this first draft and the published version.[16] Although the waitress's pregnancy remains consistent throughout all the drafts and the published version, this section, with its "round-bellied" wine bottle and the sudden, unexplained inclusion of a cat, was excised by the second draft. With the appearance of the cat, scooped up and held by the waitress, the end of "Cat in the Rain"—in which the Italian maid enters the room, holding "a big tortoise-shell cat pressed tight against her and swung down against her body" (131)[17]—reappears briefly in this story.

The three drafts of "Cross-Country Snow" also explain the mechanics of why, in the published version, George first calls Nick "Mike" (an appellation that has perplexed critics, even when Hemingway's frequent use of nicknames in writing and in life is taken into account). The story behind this editing error, which I will discuss in a moment, testifies to the increasing connectedness of these early paired stories. More importantly, it documents Hemingway's realization that their very pairing constituted an anxiety within his writerly project and probably within his own psyche. The Hemingway of 1924 would, as one might expect, face that anxiety with integrity.

Paul Smith, in *A Reader's Guide to the Short Stories of Ernest Hemingway,* succinctly explains the textual sources of the confusion: "The final typescript (KL/EH 346) and the typescript made up but not used for the 1925 edition should settle some contradictions in the characters' names. Hemingway changed the name 'Adams' to 'Nick' through the first page of the text, but missed the first reference to Mike (*Stories* 183); changed Mike to Nick throughout except for a second instance (186) and a third where someone caught it for him (188). Such instances of editorial carelessness should temper such comments as Joseph Flora's on the significance of Mike as a nickname (!) for Nick (191) or as a 'code name' like Gidge for George" (82). Although Smith explains how the mistake occurred in the published versions of the story, he does not speculate as to why Hemingway first flirted with the idea of creating a new Adams character, Mike, in this story.

But the reasons for the naming are as important as, if not more so than, the editorial mechanics behind the mistake, and the compositional pairing of the Nick Adams stories and the marriage tales illuminates these reasons. In the initial drafts of "Cross-Country Snow," and for the first time in writing the Nick Adams story sequence, he refers to his protagonist as Adams rather than Nick. This compromise, and the ensuing early draft name "Mike Adams," indicates Hemingway's reluctance to cross the previously inviolate boundary between the marriage tales and the Nick Adams stories and thus to implicate his private avatar in the complications of marriage and fatherhood—in this story, the two story sequences briefly conjoin. Hemingway's ambivalence about violating his own avenue for escape resulted in his avoiding the name Nick in the first drafts. His subsequent decision to change Mike to Nick reveals his decision to choose integrity over his self-indulgent wish for Nick to remain forever an unencumbered innocent in the Michigan Eden.

CHAPTER TWO

THE PERSONAL STORIES II

(Paris and Provence, 1926–1927)

> . . . but when you come to be successful, when you commence to earn money, when you are really successful, then your family and everybody no longer treats you like a genius, they treat you like a man who has become successful.
> —Gertrude Stein, *Picasso*

> . . . for ye are like unto whited sepulchers, which indeed appear beautiful outward, but are within full of dead men's bones . . .
> —Matthew 23:27

Between April of 1924 and September of 1926, when Hemingway began work on the next pair of marriage tale–Nick Adams stories, he had finished the stories for the 1925 collection *In Our Time,* met F. Scott Fitzgerald, written *The Torrents of Spring* (the satire that would allow him to switch publishers from Boni & Liveright to Scribner's), and written and finished authorial emendation to *The Sun Also Rises*, his roman à clef about Pamplona and the "dangerous summer" of 1925. He had also met Pauline Pfeiffer, the woman who would become his second wife, and whose relationship with him (and with his first and last wives, Hadley and Mary) would provide the basis for one of *The Garden of Eden*'s interwoven plots. Between the early period and this later dark period, Hemingway's relationship to his writing changed. He began to embed subtle layers in his writing, layers that affected the stories' meanings but would be legible only to his circle of intimates.[1] The differences between writer and author, and the respective relationships of these roles to the texts, thus began to grow.

The Dark Period Stories (Fall 1926)

The fall of 1926 was Hemingway's darkest period to date. That August, Hadley and Ernest separated; she insisted that he and Pauline spend one hundred days apart before she would give Ernest the divorce he sought. During this dark period, Hemingway wrote another pair of stories in the marriage tale–Nick Adams sequence, "Now I Lay Me," which contains the infamous burning of Dr. Adams's collections, and "A Canary for One," in which a marital separation brings the earlier marriage tales to "the conclusion they had predicted" (Smith, *Guide* 161). These paired stories, like the earlier ones, seem unrelated. But in their composition, Hemingway began to clarify and compress the connections he perceived among intergenerational homosocial betrayal (father/son; son/father), honeymoons, pregnancy, and the destruction of homes by literal and metaphorical fire. This semiotic web would inform his next stories and, much later, combine with them to form the climax of *The Garden of Eden:* the scene in which Catherine burns the suitcase containing the manuscript of David's Nick Adams–like elephant story.

The writing of three sections of "A Canary for One" deserves close attention, as their genetic evolution contributes directly to the then-developing skeins of images, motifs, and anxieties that Hemingway rearticulated in his later related works. Two of these sections contribute literally to the recurring images: the view from the train of the burning farmhouse and the women's conversation about Vevey, where the separating couple spent their honeymoon. The third section, the discussion between the unnamed American woman (their *lit salon* companion) and the wife about the relative merits of marrying foreigners and American men, resonates biographically to an extent thus far unaddressed by critics and touches on the problems of being both private writer and public author, problems that were beginning to come to the fore for Hemingway.

The first of the three relevant compositional moments occurs near the beginning of "A Canary for One." The story begins with the characters on a train heading for Paris. From the train, the American husband sees the first of two houses that evoke, respectively, intact and then broken domesticity: "The train passed very quickly a long, red stone house with a garden and four thick palm-trees with tables under them in the shade" (258). The image of the peaceful, restful red stone house gives way to another view from the train: "As it was getting dark the train passed a farmhouse burning in a field. Motor-cars were stopped along the road and bedding and things from inside the farmhouse were spread in the field. Many people were watching the house burn"

(258–59). In the first draft of this story, this section read as follows: "As it was getting dark the train passed a burning farmhouse in a field. Many people were watching it burn and motor cars were stopped along the road /.and/ and /b/Bedding and furniture were /piled/ spread in the field" (KL/EH 307, 5; /deletions/).

Hemingway's changes during this section's genetic evolution result in a slight lessening of the impact of the image (to the extent that one can soften the impact of a burning house). In this first draft, these sentences comprised their own paragraph, set apart on the page from the rest of the text. Had this distinction remained in the published version, the structure would have immediately underscored the image's importance to the story. In the next draft, however, Hemingway merged this paragraph with the previous and subsequent ones (KL/EH 308, 2), thus granting the image an impressionist aspect it would not otherwise have standing alone. As published, the image is but one of many glimpsed from the *train rapide*. Embedded within a larger paragraph in the published version, this section does not lose any of its ultimate significance; rather, the extent of its significance is harder to detect in a first reading.

A second reading, which the text structurally requires (as I will discuss in a moment), heightens the affective impact of the burning farmhouse and clarifies its function within the story as a visual projection of the internal reality of the characters' disintegrated marriage. Further, in this section, the narrator's selective reporting of what he sees portrays, in fiction, Hemingway's own practice of "[displacing] emotional content onto the terrain" (Kennedy 109, 111).[2] As modified in the second draft (KL/EH 309, 2), the scene is subtly altered to emphasize the scene as spectacle. Hemingway emphasized the voyeuristic spectators by splitting the original sentence, "Many people were watching it burn [and] motor cars were stopped along the road" (KL/EH 308, 5) into two: "Motor-cars were stopped along the road and bedding and things were spread in the field. Many people were watching the house burn" (KL/EH 309, 2). The "motor-cars" and "many people" of this latter version linguistically surround the "bedding and things." The house's most intimate contents are thus "spread" for public consumption in what was, and still could be, a fertile field. The noun "bedding" connotes the related verb and invokes the iconographic marriage bed and the manner in which it was defiled (for Hemingway, if not overtly for his narrator).

The fire despoils this marriage bed, rendering it vulnerable to visual exploitation by the "many"; by publishing this story, Hemingway similarly courted the exposure of his private guilt and Hadley's private pain. His guilt over his adulterous relationship with Pauline, the biographical source for the burning house, is never overtly addressed in the story, although it appears encoded as the catastrophic flames. Although he may have been compelled to write the story for therapeutic reasons, by spreading the Hemingways' dirty linen in public, he courted exposure. Indeed, he almost begged for it, for although his readers in 1927 obviously did not have access to the biographical details that are now generally available, Hadley and Pauline did, as would his son John when he grew old enough to understand why his father left his mother. The greater a reader's familiarity with the particulars of Hemingway's life in August and September of 1926, the greater the significance of the flames that destroy the house in the story. Two readers in particular, Hadley and Pauline, would read these details in very specific ways.

In September of 1926, the month Hemingway wrote this story, Pauline left Paris for her parents' home in Piggott, Arkansas, to endure the period of separation imposed on the lovers by Hadley. While writing "A Canary for One," Hemingway did not know if Pauline would return from her exile. His impulse to write the story stemmed at least partially from guilt over the destruction of his marriage to Hadley, but also from the fear that his relationship with Pauline might be destroyed as well.[3] Pauline and her family were actively Catholic, and the balance between her own guilt over adultery and her love for Ernest was a delicate one. During the writing of "Canary," Hemingway thus not only felt guilty but also feared that he might have risked everything for nothing.

When he decided to publish the story with unseemly haste, he may have been hedging his bets; he later, in *A Moveable Feast,* said that he had had the misfortune to love both women (and he would immortalize this misfortune in *The Garden of Eden,* which would be set in this period). *Scribner's Magazine* accepted "A Canary for One" for publication on November 11, 1926, at most two months after it was written. Hemingway thus must have submitted it almost immediately upon completion (transatlantic mail was at that time shipped by boat). When *Scribner's* accepted the story, only his immediate social circle could have broken the story's private codes (his family in the States did not know yet what was happening in Paris, although they would when the story appeared in *Men Without Women* later in 1927 [Reynolds, *Chronology* 47 and 49]).[4] His decision to publish "A Canary for One" has been judged insensitive and cruel to Hadley and John, but only because modern readers know the end of his private story—that Pauline did marry him. At the time, not even Hemingway knew how the private story—the real story—would turn out.

His haste in publishing "A Canary for One" was, though, more cunning than insensitive (although insensitive in its cunning). Had events unfolded differently, if Pauline had chosen to end their relationship, the publication of the story would have served two purposes: to sting Pauline's conscience and to publicly tender Ernest's abjection before Hadley. The story appeared in *Scribner's* in April of 1927 (Hanneman 145). Had Pauline chosen not to marry him, she would thus have read, no doubt painfully, the published story when she otherwise would have been planning their May wedding. The private message it contained for Pauline was hidden—poorly, perhaps, but hidden—from all but a few. The private message it contained for Hadley, although quite different, was equally well hidden. Had his personal life resolved otherwise, what Pauline would have read with guilt for having condemned Ernest to a "wrecked" life would have been read by Hadley as a public testimonial of his regret for and sorrow at having ruined their marriage.

His fear of having possibly destroyed three adult lives manifests in a later image in the story, the three train cars "that had been in a wreck," "splintered open and the roofs sagged in" (261). Like the bedding and nonspecific "things" in the burning farmhouse image, much of the affective impact of the three wrecked cars stems from the opening up of what was once a closed system.[5] In the original draft, Hemingway described the three cars (it is tempting to name them Ernest, Hadley, and Pauline) as follows: "The train stopped at a switch. Outside ^the window^ were three cars that had been in a wreck. They were ^splintered and^ opened up as boats are /opened up/ cross-sectioned in a/n/ ^steamship^ advertisement /in a folder/ showing the different decks or as houses are opened up by a bombardment" (KL/EH 307, 13; /deletions/; ^insertions^).

Although this section was changed in subsequent drafts, Hemingway's fixation on the "opening up" and "advertisement" aspects of the wreck combines with the subtly increased emphasis on the public spectacle of the burning farmhouse to pinpoint a central anxiety in his domestic situation—the literal publication (the making public) of his intimate life. Indeed, when he wrote the story, he was living in a studio borrowed from Gerald Murphy, a central figure in American expatriate society.[6] He had also moved some of his and Hadley's belongings through the streets of the Left Bank in a borrowed wheelbarrow. The Hemingway scandal was, like the "bedding and things" from the burning house, strewn about in public, advertising his situation in a way inimical to his Victorian Oak Park upbringing.[7]

The third section of the story that bears closer analysis here is the conversation between the American lady and the narrator's wife concerning Vevey, Switzerland, as the site for romance and early love. This honeymoon reference places "A Canary for One" at the pivot point between the earlier marriage tales

(1923–1924) and the honeymoon stories proper (1927). The American lady's daughter, to whom she is taking the canary of the title, fell in love in Vevey; the American lady, not wanting her daughter to marry a foreigner (despite his being from "a very good family" [261]), "took her away, of course" (260).

Vevey is probably the fictional representation of Schruns, Austria, where the newly married Ernest and Hadley spent a skiing holiday shortly after moving to Europe (although their honeymoon, strictly speaking, was spent at his family's cabin in Michigan), and where Pauline had vacationed with both of them at the beginning of that year (1926). The American lady says of her daughter and the Swiss man in the story's first draft, "They met skiing there in Vevey. They used to go skiing together and go on long walks together" (KL/EH 307, 12). These lines describe not only his first time in Schruns with Hadley but also the later trip with Hadley and Pauline.[8] Hemingway removed the skiing reference in the second draft (KL/EH 308, 5), possibly because Hadley would associate it too strongly with Pauline, and vice versa; reminding each of the other would have undercut his private objectives in publishing the story.

The first appearance of this honeymoon reference during the composition of "A Canary for One" occurs in an unusual place for a Hemingway draft: the verso of a page (page 12) in the handwritten first draft of the story. The use of the verso in Hemingway's early writings is exceedingly rare; he generally wrote his insertions, even long ones, between existing lines and would continue, if necessary, vertically into the margins. The insertion, which was to be included after the "skiing" line (also an insertion) on page 13, reads as follows:

"I know Vevey," said my wife. "We were there on our honeymoon."

"/How romantic that must have been,/ ^Were you really? That must have been lovely." said the American lady.

"It /is/ ^was a^ lovely ^place^," said my wife.

"Yes," said the American lady "Isn't it lovely." (KL/EH 307, 12v; /deletions/; ^insertions^)

The use of the verso for this insertion may indicate that the honeymoon idea occurred to Hemingway while rereading the first draft (as opposed to while rewriting it; he almost always made in-progress revisions, as I have said, on the recto sides). As such, the honeymoon reference in "Canary" stands as a strange kind of afterthought in Hemingway's compositional process. Although we cannot know for sure, it seems that Hemingway broke his usual composition habits and chose to reread this story in between drafts, rather than while redrafting it (the absence of verso marks in the manuscripts of other stories may support this interpretation). The unusual lack of chronological and emotional distance between the story's related biographical event and the composition of its quasi-autobiographical text may account for Hemingway's unusual attention to it. A later draft was to receive even more unusual attention (as I will discuss momentarily).

Although in the published version, the honeymoon reference survives to underscore on all levels the emotional distance the couple has traveled since their honeymoon, the first draft of this story shifts abruptly from the painful memory of the honeymoon to the view of the wrecked train cars with the line "The train stopped at a switch." This switch is the fictionalized encoding of the switching of women, resulting in the three "wrecked" lives represented visually by the wrecked train cars, with their guts exposed to the most casual observer.

Hemingway toned down this psychologically obvious passage in the published version; however, the no less psychologically suggestive prattle of the American lady regarding her successful interposition between her daughter and the suitor survived excision. When he wrote the story, Hemingway doubtless already feared what would, in fact, happen: that Pauline's mother would put pressure on her daughter to extricate herself from the situation in order to save Hemingway's marriage and family (*SL* 220). His knowledge that the Pfeiffer family was socially prominent and reasonably affluent probably combined with Pauline's job with *Vogue* in Paris to produce the women's seemingly inane conversation in "Canary" about Paris fashion houses, *vendeuses,* and the adult daughter's measurements (of which "there was not much chance of their changing now" [260], ostensibly because she had stopped growing, but also because the sterility of her thwarted love affair would not, now, result in pregnancy). Hemingway's writing of this fictional conversation thus allowed him to imagine himself the thwarted lover in a conversation between Hadley and Mrs. Pfeiffer, replete with its ironic insistence that "American men make the best husbands" (stated twice, 260).

The biographical back story of "Canary," considered carefully, suggests the emergence of a new awareness of the problems of occupying multiple roles as writer and author. (This awareness was to become an overt preoccupation in *Death in the Afternoon,* a few years later; see chapter 4.) Although the American lady objects to her daughter's lover because he is a "foreigner," two factors indicate that, biographically, writer or author might be substituted without completely giving way to speculation and fantasy.

The first of these factors is Hemingway's knowledge of the circumstances surrounding the courtship of F. Scott and Zelda Fitzgerald, whom he had met in 1925. Zelda, the daughter of a wealthy and locally important Southern family, had refused to marry Scott until he could support her in style. *This Side of Paradise* launched him to the fore of American letters, and its popularity provided him the income, or at least the promise thereof, with which to marry Zelda.[9] Hemingway's disdain for Zelda and what he saw as her interference with Scott's writing must have unsettled him, as he was living in relative penury and planning to make a socially similar match.[10]

The second factor is less easy to pinpoint biographically but is of far broader scope. Hemingway may have felt that his voluntary expatriation rendered him "foreign" to his friends from the United States; certainly, his experiences with (or at least witnessing of) the wild side of Paris, the Montparnasse of the Jazz Age, alienated him in his own mind from Oak Park.[11] Later stories, most notably "The Sea Change" (which takes as one of its subjects the uncomfortable distance of the writer from normal lives), contribute to Hemingway's understanding of himself as a writerly other. This otherness may appear encoded as "foreign" in "A Canary for One."

The American lady's problems with continental "foreigners" stems from their lack of reticence (she initially thinks the narrator and his wife are English because they lack the openness she ascribes to continental Europeans; she intends her mistake as a compliment). The problems of the writer, which figure prominently in "A Sea Change" but also, more subtly, in "Canary," involve the compulsion to make public (literally through publication) even the most painful and intimate of private experiences. Additionally, *The Sun Also Rises,* Hemingway's first novel and roman à clef, was due to be published within a month (October 22 [Hanneman 14]). While writing "A Canary for One," Hemingway may have been worried (rightly, and too late) about the reactions of the people upon whom the characters in *The Sun Also Rises* were based. Yet "A Canary for One" was another similarly exploitative project, especially considering that less than two months had passed since Ernest and Hadley had returned to Paris to set up separate residences. Guilt over his writerly compulsion to expose his own personal life (however excruciating) and to capitalize on the vulnerabilities of those closest to him, however authentic his observations, may explain why he tore the entire third draft (KL/EH 309) into several pieces, most of which he later preserved (part of the first page is missing).

This artifactual violence is nearly unique in Hemingway's extensive archive; he preserved nearly every draft of everything he wrote. The violence to which he subjected this second typescript (KL/EH 309) betrays his anger and his guilt; it informs the writing of the story but also reveals which role will prevail. Although the man tore the pages seven times, the writer preserved them and the changes made on them, preparing very shortly thereafter a clean typescript for submission to *Scribner's*. After all, as the narrator insists in the first drafts, "My wife and I are not characters in this story" (KL/EH 307, 9; 308, 3). This excised line provides a textual analog to the flames and the train wreck in that it breaks open the story, exposing and advertising the writerly text behind the authorial one.

In the last line of "A Canary for One," the reader learns that the married American couple is, like Ernest and Hadley before them, "returning to Paris to set up separate residences" (261), and that the story has chronicled their last moments together. This last line requires that one reread the story in order to appreciate the irony of their conversation with the American woman, and pertinence of the narration of various scenes that the husband has seen from the train.[12] Hemingway thus forces his readers to relive the experience with excruciating awareness, just as he did while writing.

In this 1926 story, Hemingway came as close as he had yet to acknowledging the deep discomfort he felt at making the private public (which happens in any divorce, and in all his Personal writing).[13] (He would pathologize this discomfort much later.) He also began, metaphorically, to play with fire as his symbol of choice for the deliberate betrayal and destruction of the emotional bonds within a marriage. In the earliest fragment of what became "Now I Lay Me" (KL/EH 618), young Nicky (Hemingway originally wrote "Ernie," the only place in his manuscripts where he makes this error) assists his mother with the burning of his father's prized personal possessions (including the nicely Freudian snakes that his naturalist father had preserved in jars), only to realize later that by helping his mother he has betrayed his father. Both the marriage tale theme and the theme of intergenerational, father-son betrayal will reemerge, newly fashioned, in the stories Hemingway wrote while on his honeymoon with Pauline in May 1927.

The Early Honeymoon Fiction (May 1927)

During the writing of the early honeymoon fiction ("Hills Like White Elephants" and "Ten Indians"), the schism between writer and author grew even wider and had increasingly serious repercussions in the texts. In these stories, especially "Hills Like White Elephants," the writer-author split reached its most profound distance to date. In addition, the concurrent composition of "Hills" and "Ten Indians" illuminates a highly personal linkage between honeymoons and fatherhood, between romantic commitment and homosocial betrayal. When considered in light of the story of Hadley, the lost valise of manuscripts, and her subsequent pregnancy, these two stories, taken together, mark an early milestone in Hemingway's developing personal semiotic of love and father-hood, signified by suitcases and elephants (both of which connect directly to romantic and paternal commitment in "Hills Like White Elephants") and food (which serves as inadequate nourishment in counterpoint to romantic and paternal betrayal in the final version of "Ten Indians"). A much older Hemingway would return to this honeymoon, these stories, and these specific images in *The Garden of Eden.* Just as writing Nick Adams into the Michigan woods allowed Hemingway access to the Edenic memories of his adolescent freedom, drama-tizing his Provençal honeymoon in *The Garden of Eden* would return an aging Hemingway to the time when he most enjoyed writing.

During the 1927 honeymoon, Hemingway was able finally to finish "Ten Indians," the ending of which had eluded him for over a year and a half. In this final version, Nick's father literally stumbles upon Nick's girlfriend, Prudie (the tenth Indian of the title), with another male while Nick is in town for the Fourth of July with friends. Nick returns home after seeing the other nine passed out drunk on the side of the road, whereupon his father tells him about Prudie's infidelity. Two earlier drafts of the ending exist, both of which were written during the long deterioration of his first marriage (Smith, *Guide* 197). The first draft, the 1925 Chartres version, was written in a French school notebook, or *cahier* (KL/EH 202c; David Bourne, in *The Garden of Eden,* writes his own Nick Adams-like story in a similar *cahier* whilst on his own Provençal honeymoon). In this draft, Nick Adams functions as a witness to his girlfriend Prudie's central but unidentified trauma (Smith, *Guide* 197). In the 1926 Madrid version, Prudie loses her sympathetic role and takes on that of Nick's sexual and romantic betrayer, the role she would play in each sub-sequent version. In this version, the affective focus shifts briefly to Nick but is complicated by an additional shift, at the end, to his father, who has revealed Prudie's unfaithfulness. After Nick goes to bed, Dr. Adams confronts feelings of inadequacy as a father (he prays, "Dear God, for Christ's sake keep me from ever telling things to a kid" [KL/EH 728 and 729; Smith, *Guide* 197–98]) and, perhaps, as a husband (he lies "crossways in the big double bed to take up as much room as he could. He was a very lonely man" [KL/EH 728 and 729; Smith, *Guide* 198]). The story takes place in the Michigan cabin where Ernest and Hadley had, like Hemingway's parents before them, spent their honeymoon,[14] which strongly suggests the possibility that, for Dr. Adams, this empty bed was his honeymoon bed.

The honeymoon, or Provence, version of "Ten Indians" (KL/EH 727 and 730) places Nick, and Nick alone, squarely in the story's affective foreground and reduces Dr. Adams's role to one of witness, messenger, and inadequate nurturer. This final version clarifies Dr. Adams's relationship to the concept of betrayal in this story: he is no longer even suggested as the object of betrayal. He has become, exclusively, its agent. Not only is he the messenger of bad news, but his inadequacy as a parent compounds his implication: he can offer his emotionally injured son nothing but an extra piece of pie by way of comfort. In contrast to the kinship Nick sees in the Gardner family at the beginning of the story, the Adams family members exist in emotionally sterile cocoons, alone even when physically together.

Hemingway's honeymoon version of "Ten Indians" reorients the intergenerational betrayal evident in the burning episode of "Now I Lay Me" from the betrayal of father by son to the betrayal of son by father, in both cases because of a woman. In "Now I Lay Me," the son Nicky/Ernie is cast by his mother as an unwitting accomplice in a betrayal; in "Ten Indians," the father, Dr. Adams, is cast by Hemingway as a conflicted accomplice in a similar betrayal. Both betrayals hint strongly at emasculation (Mrs. Adams burns, among other things, Dr. Adams's collection of flint arrowheads as well as the snakes; Prudie "threshes around" in the woods with another male), and both betrayals are homosocial. In the honeymoon writing, however, the direction is reversed: in the honeymoon, father betrays son. Hemingway's reinscription of guilt away from the son and onto the father during these months is biographically fitting. During this dark period, he neglected to inform his parents of his separation from Hadley; during the honeymoon, he had yet to inform them of the wedding. This minor betrayal pales in comparison to the larger one that Hemingway, as a father, had perpetrated on his own son because of a woman: by leaving Hadley for Pauline in 1926, Hemingway had betrayed not only his wife but three-year-old John as well. Young Nick, in these stories, thus figures not only as Hemingway's avatar but implies Hemingway's strong identification with his own young son. In the 1924 "Cross-Country Snow," Hemingway had reluctantly implicated Nick Adams in marriage and fatherhood; in these later Nick Adams stories, Nick became even less of an escape for him. Perhaps because of this, Hemingway would soon abandon the Nick stories and not return to them for twenty years, in the writing of *The Garden of Eden* and "The Last Good Country."[15]

"Hills Like White Elephants," the marriage tale in the honeymoon pair, seems to connect with "Ten Indians" in that the theme of father-child betrayal reappears in the characters' debate whether or not to abort an unexpected pregnancy. "Hills" also introduces, biographically, the last of the four early psychological issues that will reemerge, transformed, in *The Garden of Eden:* gender switching, or cross-gendered experimentation.[16]

In order to identify the deeply hidden gender switching in the writerly text of "Hills," I must explicate the story, as it was published, in some detail. The unnamed man advocates the abortion; Jig, his girlfriend, is open to imagining a future that includes their child. Critics have nearly universally read the ending of this story as indicating that the man wins the struggle and that Jig and the unborn child lose. But "Hills" can be read, with equal accuracy, in two ways. The traditional critical reading has the story ending either with the abortion or a breakup; another viewpoint can see the couple choosing to stay together and not to have the abortion. The traditional reading is supported, almost perfectly, by the published text (what I term the authorial version); the second is supported equally well by the writerly text represented in the story's only extant manuscript and its compositional context.

"Hills Like White Elephants" stands as perhaps the earliest textual evidence of Hemingway's own cross-gendering experiments, in which his own metaphorically biographical role in the story is played not by the man, but by the woman, Jig. Because *The Garden of Eden* relies so heavily on this text and the writing of it, and because my reading of this story as cross-gendered autobiography diametrically opposes that of nearly every other critic since the story's publication, I will provide an extensive close reading of both the published (authorial) version and its single extant manuscript (the writer's text) in this chapter before considering its contributions to the later novel in the next.

As a starting point, consider the following passage from *The Garden of Eden:* "David wished that he had brought a casting rod and spoons so that he might cast out across the flow of water" (7). The term "spoons" provides a nearly invisible link to one of the earlier stories, "Hills Like White Elephants." A spoon in fishing refers to a bright, concave metal disk around which fish hooks are attached. Another term for such a device, which functions as both lure and hook, is a "jig."

In "Hills Like White Elephants," Hemingway names the young woman who is considering an abortion Jig. From the perspective of her lover, who initially desires neither commitment nor complications (who, rather, has an immature wish to undo the pregnancy so that they will be as they were before), the fishing connotation of her name is particularly apt. To him, Jig really is a bright lure with potentially dangerous hooks. The American man in "Hills" would agree, at least initially, with Bill's warning (in "The Three-Day Blow") that "Once a man's married, he's absolutely bitched" (90).

"Hills Like White Elephants" shares with *The Garden of Eden* not only its "jig" reference but, more importantly, its intimate connection to a Grau du Roi honeymoon, having been written during that of Ernest and Pauline

Hemingway in 1927. Furthermore, it shares *The Garden of Eden*'s most heavily charged (if somewhat unlikely) images: suitcases and elephants. Finally, it marks a complete schism between the authorial text and that of the writer. Despite the fact that the words are the same in the authorial and writerly texts, the two end differently—and their equally well-supported endings are mutually exclusive.

Stanley Renner's essay, "Moving to the Girl's Side of 'Hills Like White Elephants,'" offers a revolutionary reading of the published story's conclusion: "[Jig] decides not to have an abortion, and her companion, though not without strong misgivings, acquiesces in her decision" (27). This conclusion becomes clear for Renner through "a study of Hemingway's characterization of the pregnant girl" (27), which he traces through five stages, or "movements," in the text. Although Renner's conclusion differs strikingly from that of every other critic in the story's seventy-plus-year history (who argue either that Jig concedes and undergoes the abortion despite her own desires or that she leaves her intractable lover), Renner is strongly supported by a biographical detail that critical responses to the story neglect: the dedication of the manuscript to Pauline Pfeiffer, "Mss for Pauline—Well, well, well" (KL/EH 473, 12). Paul Smith wonders at the apparent paradox between this dedication and the story's ending, as traditionally read, especially given Pauline's Catholic faith (*Guide* 206). Michael Reynolds notes the "disturbing fact that Hemingway completed the story while on his honeymoon with Pauline" in May 1927 (*Chronology* 7–8).

Yet neither Smith nor Reynolds develops this evocative thread, and beyond their statement of fact and expression of puzzlement,[17] biographical information is absent in critical responses to the story, an absence most likely due to the lack of evidence that Pauline (or, for that matter, Hadley) ever had an abortion. That this story lacks the evident autobiographical basis of the earlier marriage tales is apparently so obvious that it does not warrant mention.

But questions remain. Why would Hemingway give to the Catholic Pauline, his new bride, a story in which either a relationship is destroyed or a pregnancy terminated? This is especially troubling given that the date of composition indicates that this manuscript may have been a wedding present, from husband to wife.[18] What to make of the fact that Hemingway himself referred to this story as one of his "hard" stories, implying in a letter to his editor Maxwell Perkins that "hard" meant "better"?[19]

Renner's aggressive reading of the story's physiospatial rhetoric partially answers these questions. If the story does not end tragically, then it is indeed hard—much harder than can be accounted for by the mere omission of the word "abortion." Further, if the man does "capitulate," as Renner argues (28), then the matter of the manuscript as wedding present loses some of (but not all) its shock value. If one keeps the circumstances of the story's production firmly in mind while reading the story, Renner's persuasive argument for resolution is strengthened. Yet why have generations of readers, from Dorothy Parker to Allen Josephs,[20] responded so emphatically with exactly the opposite interpretation—that the story is a tragedy? In order to resolve questions arising from the story's ambiguity, e.g., why the published story seems to support at least two equal and opposite readings of its ending, I propose first to examine the textual elements that create that ambiguity, and then to marshal archival and biographical information to support and extend Renner's general claims.

Both sides of the critical debate (Renner, opposing literally all other critics) have textual support—perhaps because of the near balance Hemingway ascribes to the rhetorical sides in the story. Nearly everything in the story, even the white elephants of the title, supports two equally likely but opposite meanings. A first denotation of white elephants is unwanted junk. But not just any unwanted junk; this is the junk you bring to a white elephant sale because although you find it worthless, someone else might not. Sure enough, at the second mention of white elephants in the narrative, Jig finds the hills "lovely" (212). An additional, historical exegesis of a white elephant embraces the term's positive and negative connotations: a white elephant is a gift bringing both honor and ruin to its recipient.[21] At first glance, it means one thing. At second, it means two—not one of two, but one and two. Honor and ruin.

The story's valley setting is bisected, "this" side (the infertile side, "brown and dry," with "no trees"), and "the other" side (the fertile side, with fields of grain, the river, and trees), by not one but "two lines of rails," between which the couple sits "at a table in the shade" (211). The setting is introduced in two stages, first within the opening paragraph, where we are given the bleak view; the second describes the "lovely" view (213). At first glance, the valley is one way: barren. Later, we learn that it is two: both barren and fertile, simultaneously. So which hills are like white elephants? The narrative states that "the hills across the valley . . . were long and white," and that "on this side there [were] . . . no trees" (211). When Jig defends her choice of simile, however, she states that she "meant the coloring of their skin through the trees" (212). There are no trees on "this" side; she therefore must mean the trees she remembers seeing before sitting down, which have yet to appear in the text. Her companion does not look, but if he did, he, "close against the side of the station" (211), would only see the barren side. Valleys are valleys by virtue of lying between two lines of hills; by definition and by textual determination the "hills like white elephants" must be on both sides, but only after a careful reading and wrestling with the word "across" does this become clear.[22] Of course the hills lie across the valley—the station is between them; whichever way you look, they are "across" (211, 212). The hills on both sides, then, are "like white elephants."

Just as the valley lies between the two lines of hills, the station sits between two lines of rails, presumably representing two directions of travel ("to Madrid" and "to Barcelona"). One line is on the fertile side; one on the barren side. When the man moves the suitcases across, to the "other tracks" (214), we first assume that he moves them in order to put them onto the train to Madrid (which at that point is "coming in five minutes" [214]). But those tracks are on the "other" side, the "fertile" side, which we know from the fact that Jig moves to the end of the station to look at it, where she sees the "river," across the valley, "through the trees" (213). Why, in a story in which every detail of setting is so carefully determined—even overdetermined—would the train headed toward the abortion come on the "fertile" side of the valley? This leads, of course, to two additional questions. Why, at the end of the story, is Jig smiling? And why does the American man need an *anis* in the bar when his beer awaits at the table?

The first time one reads the story, one assumes that Jig's smile is forced, that she is being submissive and conciliatory; conversely, one might also assume that she smiles because she has decided to leave her lover and have the baby on her own (Hannum 47; Renner 27). But once one remembers which side is which (by remembering Jig's movement to look toward the distance "through the trees"), Renner's argument that she smiles because the man has capitulated (34) also makes sense—even more so when one remembers that her first smile, to the Spanish waitress, is "to thank her" (214) nonverbally, in the only language they share. Jig and the man also appear to share only one language, that same nonverbal language (which comes as no surprise given the probable basis of their relationship). If the first smile means "I don't speak your language, but thank you," the second, which follows so hard upon the first, may mean exactly the same thing, in which case the third and final smile could easily follow suit: "Thank you for telling me with your actions what you could not communicate in words." At first her smile means one thing; later, perhaps another. Unlike the inclusive meanings of "across" and "white elephants," however, the two possible meanings of the man's moving the suitcases and of Jig's smiles are mutually exclusive. Either they are taking the train to have the abortion or they are not. Either Jig smiles to thank him honestly or to mask her true emotions. How are we to discern the difference?

Hemingway has not, for all his overdetermination of setting, clearly designated either set of rails "to Madrid."

Hemingway provides a possible clue with the timing. We know that the train is due "in five minutes" (214) and that it will stop for two (211). The man, therefore, has seven minutes to announce that he will move the suitcases, move them, look "up the tracks" and "not see the train," go into the bar, order an *anis,* drink it, look at the people "waiting reasonably" while drinking, come out through the curtain, and rejoin Jig at the table (to "finish the beer," as she states earlier [214]). There is absolutely no way to know for sure whether this takes more or less than seven minutes, and Hemingway, again, does not say. This information may or may not be valuable—another potential white elephant.

What do we know for sure? The story is almost perfectly symmetrical. In its first section, the setting is established in the narration, introducing "this" barren half of the valley. The couple sits together in a "shadow" (211) at a table and is interrupted briefly by the waitress. After looking at the bamboo curtain and holding two of its strands in her hand, Jig announces her concession to the man's wishes that she terminate her pregnancy, rises, and moves alone to the end of the station. The second section of the story, like the first, begins with a description of setting (now, of the other, fertile side of the valley). Many of the elements present in the first section are repeated in the second, but with the active roles reversed: Jig sees a second shadow (213), the couple again sits at the table, the waitress interrupts, and the man looks at nearby objects (the two bags). He then moves, alone, to the other side, carrying the bags; pauses to look and ruminate; and then rejoins Jig at the table. The two then, presumably, board the train to Madrid for the abortion. The story's physical action is "perfectly simple" (213). Or is it?

Two actions are missing from the narration and thus from the description. Although Hemingway does not tell us when Jig drops the strands of beads, he does not need to. Their release must occur before she leaves the table; the most likely moment is at her climactic line "Then I'll do it. Because I don't care about me" (213). If she underscores these words with such an action, however unconsciously, her action-oriented companion may be more likely to notice that something is amiss.

What Hemingway does need to tell us, and what has gone unremarked since the story's publication in 1927, is that at the narrative fulcrum, the man joins Jig at the end of the station. When Jig laments, "we could have all this," the man responds, "What did you say?" Smith notes at this point that "many have wondered why she does not stalk off" and leave him (*Guide* 211). Why indeed? Because the man's question suggests, as does so much else in the story, two mutually exclusive interpretations: either he has not been paying attention and is therefore a selfish cad (which he has certainly proved to this point), or else he quite legitimately does not hear her. The next several lines of dialogue evince such tight stichomythia that he apparently must hear her lament, but the text later reveals that this is a false assumption, the result of narrative misdirection. After the man says, "You mustn't feel that way," "*they* sat down at the table" (214; emphasis added). For both to sit, both must have been standing. The man therefore must have moved during the dialogue. But when? And why?

The reader must work backward through the text. The only plausible moment for him to move is as he asks that difficult question, "What did you say?" Prior to this line, Jig is alone; subsequent to it the dialogue is so tight that motion is not only improbable but illogical. The pronoun "they" reveals that the man's movement is, like Poe's purloined letter, hidden in plain sight. The man's movement changes his "Come on back" from an imperative to a plea. If the question "What did you say?" is not damnably insensitive, as Smith has suggested, but rather a mere request for repetition (and he does want to know what she said; he moves to hear her), what else may we, disgusted like Jig by the man's apparent callousness, have missed?

We have missed the beginning of understanding that the man's words have begun to evince, and which his motion to join her underscores. Reading backward yet again, we can scan no farther for this beginning than the exchange at which Jig drops the beads: "I'll do it. Because I don't care about me," prompting the man's question "What do you mean?" (213) Prior to this question, he has expressed interest only in a short-term (but permanent) solution to what he perceives as an "unhappy" problem (212). As Renner argues (31), when confronted with "I don't care about me," he may begin, however dimly, to perceive that what he sees as expedient, Jig sees as a sacrifice. If "I don't care about me" jolts his complacency, and if his retort, "Well, I care about you," is honest, then the remainder of the story should reveal his attempts to reopen communication and to convey a willingness to listen to her side. As Pamela Smiley notes, he can speak only his own limited language, relying on "the repetition of key words and phrases" (9), and he cannot understand Jig's. He can, however, read her actions. He will discover that his earlier insincerity has contaminated the very words he must now employ to elicit an opposite response. His efforts will be frustrated even further by Jig's reasonable (given his stance thus far) resistance to his words. He must transform himself from antagonist to hero in slightly less than two pages of narrative and slightly less than thirty minutes of dramatic time.

Returning to the stichomythic dialogue (from "What did you say?" to "We'll wait and see" [213]), the evidence for a shift in the man's rhetorical position appears almost immediately. The dialogue begins in the indicative mood ("We can/can't have everything"). After Jig's statement that "once they take it away you can never get it back," the man breaks the indicative can-can't pattern with "They haven't taken it away" (213). He is thus attempting to re-open the discussion. This is so subtle that Jig (and many readers) miss this verbal "action." His tactic fails; he continues to try to convince her that the debate is still open with two statements, "I don't want you to do anything that you don't want to do—" and "But you've got to realize—" These lines unfortunately echo, nearly verbatim, his earlier, insincere words: "But I don't want you to do it if you really don't want to" (213). Jig interrupts both later statements, having already heard too many variations on these words to trust them now.

From this moment, the story develops in an intricate calculus of the repetition of and variations on existing elements. The characters resume their original positions at the table, and much of the action from the story's opening section is repeated: one character looks at things, one does not; one character tries to communicate, the other refuses to listen; the waitress interrupts a tense moment by bringing beer; the man translates for Jig; one character moves to the other side, and the narrative voice speaks from that character's perspective. Now, though, the couple's respective positions in the spatial and communication dynamics are reversed.

Jig has spent the entire story looking at her surroundings (hills, ground, curtain, fields, and shadow); the man has yet to look directly at anything. He does so now: first at her, then at the table, the bags, the tracks, and, finally, the people in the bar (214). Jig, in this second section, does not appear to look at anything. Just as the man is the one who looks, he is the one who now confronts the urgency of their situation and who must attempt to communicate this urgency to her, just as she tried (and failed) to do initially. Her orientation has been spatial (imaginative) throughout; his must be temporal (goal directed): whereas she perceived the possibility of "the whole world" (213), he can only perceive the ticking of the clock, the train's timetable, and the rising odds against resolution.

Unfortunately, at this point in the story, we and Jig are confronted with a veritable plethora of indefinite pronouns, nine of which are obviously indefinite ("it") and one of which in its first instance appears to be definite ("we") but by its second, at least in the manuscript, is quite the opposite:

> "You've got to realize . . . that I don't want you to do it if you don't want to. I'm
> perfectly willing to go through with it if it means anything to you."
> "Doesn't it mean anything to you? We could get along."
> "Of course it does. But I don't want anybody but you. I don't want any one else. And I
> know it's perfectly simple."
> "Yes, you know it's perfectly simple."
> "It's all right for you to say that but I do know it." (214)

Two lines from this section of dialogue proved the most elusive to Hemingway as he reworked them through no fewer than four complete versions between the first draft and publication (KL/EH 473, 10). The published version reads:

> "Doesn't it mean anything to you? We could get along."
> "Of course it does. But I don't want anybody but you. I don't want anyone else. And I know it's perfectly simple." (214)

In the first draft, this section of dialogue reads two ways:

> 1. "It doesn't mean anything to you?"
> "Of course it does. But it's just a question of expediency. And I know it's perfectly simple."
> 2. "Doesn't it mean anything to you?"
> "Of course it does. But I don't want anybody but you. I don't want anyone else. I know how the other thing is. And I know it's perfectly simple."

By the end of the first draft, Jig's initially strong accusation "It doesn't mean anything to you?" has been weakened slightly, but the man's attitude remains essentially unchanged. Both first draft versions indicate that his position never waivers.

The second-sitting revisions, the final ones made on the manuscript, also contain two versions of this section (the latter of which matches the published text).[23] The first raises the abortion debate to a new level, one that recognizes the baby as a real third person:

3. "Doesn't it mean anything to you? Three of us could get along."
"Of course it does. And I know we could."

Hemingway rejected this version in favor of the more ambiguous published text, rightly excising Jig's reference to the "three of us" as a flaw—not necessarily of content, but of effect. The phrase is too direct, too obvious, and represents too efficient a form of communication to be consistent with these characters. "To explain is to destroy," as Nakjavani notes in his investigation into Hemingway's style (43). Even so, Hemingway tried these same three words again during the second sitting at a later point in the story, but this time in the man's lines:

> He did not say anything but looked at /her/ the bags against the wall of the station. There were /stickers/ labels on them from all the hotels where they had /spent nights/ stopped.
> "But I don't want you to," he said, "I don't care anything about it. / *Three of us could get*/" (KL/EH 473, 10–11; emphasis added; /deletions/)

Thus after "He did not say anything," he does say something—too much and too directly, judging from the fact that Hemingway did not even complete the sentence before crossing it out. Although Hemingway's oft-quoted assertion regarding the lingering affective resonance of "things left out" must be invoked with caution, the rhetorical shift from "expediency" to "three of us" is diametric and total. Of all the things "left out," or at least crossed out, of all Hemingway's stories, these three words may be the most startling, as they support without question the existence of an interpretive possibility that Renner alone has articulated.

The man has been misunderstood in his first foray toward the language of commitment. His reply to Jig's sarcasm, "but I do know it," indicates both that he does know what he is trying to say, and that he knows with equal certainty that he is failing miserably. When she asks that they "please please please please please please please stop talking," the man is forced to comply to prove the sincerity of his claim that he would "do anything for you" (214). He is dutifully silent "but looked at the bags" (214). This sentence could as easily have read "*and* looked at the bags"; the conjunction "but" serves to link his consideration of the bags to what he would say had he not bound himself unwittingly to silence.

The labels remind him of their nights together and spur him to attempt communication once more: "But I don't want you to . . . I don't care anything about it" (214). Although in the published text, the man certainly does not continue by asserting that the three of them could get along, the repetition of "but" in this passage indicates that he knows the matter is too important for him to keep silent. Once again, though, the effect of his words is the opposite of what he intends. "I don't care anything about it" is a terrible rhetorical fumble. Neither Jig, who threatens to scream, nor the reader, who might want to, can locate an antecedent for that crucial "it"—which in the manuscript refers to neither abortion nor baby, but to his earlier stance in the debate. Frustrated and overwhelmed, he is capitulating—reluctantly, to be sure, but he is finally conceding.

The story's ultimate ambiguity resides in the nearly perfect balance Hemingway crafted in the manuscript between the representative sides, both spatial and rhetorical. A collation of the manuscript (KL/EH 473) with the text of the first edition (the 1927 edition of *Men Without Women*) reveals that the nearly overwhelming ambiguity in the story was the result of emendations made during a second writing session, which included the man's surprising "three of us." This set of emendations reveals a striking difference between the narrative in its first draft and that which became the published version.

In the first draft, the story reads as many have read the published text: the man's character and attitude remain static throughout, and Jig must either defer to his judgment regarding the abortion or end the relationship. During the second sitting, however, Hemingway made the following subtle changes, which, taken together, allow for the interpretation Renner proposes. To Jig's apology, "I just meant the coloring of their skin," he added "through the trees" (KL/EH 473, 5). After "It's the only thing that's made us unhappy," he added "The girl looked /away/ at the bead curtain, /and/ put her hand out and took hold of two of the strings of beads" (KL/EH 473, 6). He added "The shadow of a cloud moved across the field of grain and she saw the river through the trees" (KL/EH 473, 8). He changed the imperative, paternalistic "But you must realize" to the more pleading "you've got to realize" (KL/EH 473, 9). He reworked the difficult dialogue, added a "please," and nearly let the cat out of the bag with "three of us" (KL/EH 473, 10–11). He also added Jig's second smile, her response to "I'd better take the bags over to the other side of the station" (KL/EH 473, 11). By adding a few phrases and sentences, a please, and a smile, Hemingway made an alternative ending possible.

As a set, these second-sitting emendations heighten the story's ambiguity. Why do we care about the trees? They orient us within the setting and cement both characters' perceptions spatially. The beads? Because we and the man can see Jig considering her options and deciding. The addition of the line containing the cloud's shadow provides not only an evocative image (potentially ominous, from Jig's perception, but potentially bringing the cool relief of rain to a parched valley) but, more importantly, reminds us about the trees, in case we missed them the first time (and we need to know where the trees are, so we know that both lines of hills are "like white elephants"). Why a second smile? Because it links her first and her third, and because it provides us with her immediate response to the man's decision to move the bags. Is she saying thank you again, and for much more than just carrying the heavy bags? The bags are "heavy" indeed if they contain not only their literal contents but also their possible metaphorical meaning. Prior to the man's movement, they suggest the superficiality of the relationship: they bear only the surface symbols of a peripatetic existence. As the man carries them, however, they are two, they are full, and they are heavy. They now have internal content and heft and bear a closer affinity to the weighty commitment of parenthood.

As the man moves the bags to the other side (and, not incidentally, into the light), the narrative voice shifts to his perspective and indicates his distance from the train (which he does not see). This underscores his distance from the people who will, unlike himself, "reasonably" board the train for which they have been waiting, rather than some later train that will take them into an uncertain future. From his perspective, abortion would have been the "reasonable" course of action. The recent debate must have felt anything but "reasonable" to him. But he has learned that his perspective is just that: his. As he sits in the interior space, which Kozikowski obliquely associates with the womb (108), one wonders why he is there, if not to steady his nerves and to let the idea of impending fatherhood start to sink in.

Smith notes that the first draft of this section reads quite differently from the published text: "There must be some actual world. There must be some place you could touch where people were calm and reasonable. Once it had all been as simple as this bar" (Smith, *Guide* 205; KL/EH 473, 2). Smith asserts that "They were all waiting reasonably for the train," with which Hemingway replaced these deleted lines during the second sitting, functions as a "[reduction of] the whole perception to the inserted sentence with its metaphoric adverb" (205). This interpretation is consistent with the reading that proposes that the man's "benighted vision" remains unaltered, yet by making this second-sitting change, Hemingway lends "reasonably" more rhetorical weight than Smith suggests. It may function not as a "reducing" metaphor, but rather as a metaphor for the distance traveled by the man, who literally turns his back on reason when he rejoins Jig outside. From his perspective, he has been hooked and landed by Jig, in keeping with her name. Although several critics have discussed the relevance of "Jig" most extensively (O'Brien 12; Abdoo 240), one definition is consistently and surprisingly left out. According to the 1913 edition of *Webster's Revised Unabridged Dictionary,* a jig is not only a dance, a mechanical sheath, etc. (as critics have noted); it is also "a trolling bait, consisting of a bright spoon and a hook attached" (800). That Hemingway would be unaware of the connotational possibilities of "bright lure" and "hook" to Jig's name is highly unlikely, especially in light of David Bourne's wish for such a device in *The Garden of Eden* (7).

In response to the white elephant aspect of their situation, the man may have done the honorable thing, but the lingering negative affect derives from his focus on their previous life as having been ruined. When the man emerges from the bar, the "three of them" have barely survived the struggle in this isolated valley arena. His movements and her smiles are actions, in the language of the arena, the language that does not require words, and the only language in which the two communicate fluently. This is not to say that the story presents the reader with a blissful vision of the union or its future. It does not. Physiospatial communication may avert the unnecessary termination of an unplanned but not entirely unwelcome pregnancy, yet gendered miscommunication will extend beyond the closing of the arena into real life. The two will have to learn to communicate verbally; the prognosis can be only guarded at best.

A partial answer, then, to the disturbing question of why Hemingway gave Pauline this story within three weeks of their Catholic wedding is that Pauline, reading the manuscript, could see instantly what has taken so long to reconstruct here: that not only does the American man change his mind halfway through the story, but that Ernest Hemingway did too, halfway through the writing. He initially wrote the story as most people interpret it and then laid over it a nearly transparent layer consisting of a few minute changes that transform the initially simple story entirely. The subtlety of this transformation nearly disappears from the story as it was published, among others in the already-titled *Men Without Women.* But Pauline, on her honeymoon in 1927, had access to the writerly text, and as such to two sources of information that a reader holding just the published text does not. The first, of course, was the twelve-page manuscript, visual evidence of the transformation that Hemingway had wrought on the story. What had been a "perfectly simple" story in the first draft had become a narrative palimpsest, an almost perfectly symmetrical and diabolically ambiguous story, one that can end with nearly equal certainty in tragic disunity or Aristotelian comic unity. Pauline's second advantage was her intimate knowledge of what the word "abortion" meant to Hemingway within the context of their relationship—in other words, in the mind of the writer.

During the writing of "Hills Like White Elephants," he deviated from his then-usual composition method, which was to prepare his own typescripts and to make emendations as he prepared various typed drafts. By December 6, 1926, he had broken his typewriter (Bruccoli, *The Only Thing That Counts* 53), and he presumably did not bring the one he borrowed to Grau du Roi. His own had been damaged, perhaps, by heavy key pounding as he wrote desperate, forbidden letters to Pauline during the bleak hundred-day separation initially prescribed by Hadley as a condition for divorce.

These letters and cables, several of which are unfinished (KL/EH Correspondence), reveal Hemingway's despair as communications from Pauline grew sporadic and finally stopped altogether. He knew from her sister Virginia (Jinny) that their mother, with whom Pauline was staying in Piggott, Arkansas, was preying on Pauline's guilt at destroying Hemingway's marriage and family.[24] Unable to control Piggott from Paris, Hemingway waited, in a "black depression" (*SL* 234), for Pauline's decision either to return to marry him in Paris or to accept a job in New York. He would not know her decision, for sure, until she sailed.

Hemingway waged a long-distance written campaign against and for Pauline's conscience. In his letters, one can trace the evolution of one of his most elusive metaphors—the metaphor that was to be left out of "Hills Like White Elephants." The metaphor originated in his encoding of their relationship as a nascent body. In his letter of November 12, 1926, he attempts to persuade her that the stakes of her decision outweigh the obvious sins of adultery and divorce; he implies that their reunion is a matter of life and death: "It was certain that your mother would feel badly about your marrying some one [*sic*] who was divorced, about breaking up a home, about getting into a mess—and it is certain too that silent disapproval is the most *deadly*" (*SL* 220; emphasis added).

Hemingway rhetorically alleviates adultery and divorce by renaming them "mess" and then by juxtaposing that relatively benign noun with the weighty descriptive "deadly." This charged adverb marks the conception of what was initially a relatively simple metaphor: for their relationship to be in "deadly" peril, it must be somehow "alive." It is mortally threatened by Pauline's apparent decision to break off the relationship: "evidently we are to be smashed by choice—our own free choice—in a grievous matter, with deliberate and full consent" (*SL* 222).

Hemingway next elaborates this metaphor by giving the relationship a body. Under the conditions of this evolving metaphor, love can potentially realize embodiment (metaphysical birth) through the motion of bodies (in this case, Pauline) across space (the Atlantic) toward union (marriage/intercourse). The strange alchemy of Hemingway's creative mind will resolve this traditional erotic vision into one of his most subtle works by capitalizing on his having placed the burden of the metaphorical tenor, relationship as body, on the improbable vehicle, surgery: "But I won't and I won't think about it and maybe you'll come back and maybe there will be something left of you and maybe we'll have a little guts and not try self sacrifices in the middle of surgical operations and maybe we'll come through and maybe and maybe and maybe and maybe" (*SL* 222).

The "surgical operations" in question here seem to refer both to the divorce from Hadley and the separation from Pauline, "self sacrifices" indicating Pauline's possible inclination to listen to her mother (*SL* 220) and perhaps (as Hemingway feared) to end their relationship.

Hemingway combines the "surgical operation" motif with the idea of "sacrifice" in a later letter, dated December 3, as he recasts Pauline's apparent decision to stay in the United States as a decision to "abort" their embryonic relationship: "You see Pfife I think that when two people love each other [going away from each other] works almost as bad as an *abortion*. . . . But the deliberate keeping apart when all you have is each other does something bad to you and lately it has me all shot to hell inside" (*SL* 234; emphasis added).

Hemingway here implies that their relationship is (and thus the two of them are) metaphorically pregnant; he asserts that his pain, his fear that Pauline will reject him, is akin to that of a pregnant mother who is shot in the womb. Although this is certainly melodramatic, Hemingway's self-representation as somehow pregnant underscores the possibility that as a writer he considered the couple in "Hills Like White Elephants" a very heavily fictionalized, cross-gendered representation of his and Pauline's relationship during the fall of 1926. Two people in love, his vision asserts, create between them a metaphorical pregnancy; to sacrifice it is to abort the union. Pauline finally decided against sacrifice in favor of union. On December 30, 1926, she sailed for France (Kert 198), moving her suitcases to the other side of the Atlantic. The wedding took place in Paris on May 10, 1927.

Furthermore, biographer Carlos Baker asserts (fortuitously, but problematically) that Hemingway "began the story in the first person," identifying the author's March 31, 1927, letter to Fitzgerald as the source for one of the story's images: "We sat at a table in the shade of the station" (595n). Although line was typed onto the page before Hemingway reused the paper for the letter and thus is disconnected from the actual text of the letter,[25] Smith notes that the same letter also contains the "Well, well, well" phrase from the dedication (*Guide* 206; *SL* 249). Further, the text of the letter itself contains the lines, "Pauline is *fine* and back from America. I've been in love with her so damned long that certainly is *fine* to see a little something of her" (*SL* 249; emphasis added). The "black depression" is over and, although he sounds a little bitter about it, there's nothing wrong with him. He, like Jig at the end of the story, feels fine.

Well, well, well, indeed.

Most readers do not, of course, have Pauline's advantages of having read Hemingway's letters to her and of reading the holograph manuscript. Only scholars familiar with Smith's work have any knowledge of the dedication, which has never appeared with the published story. "Hills Like White Elephants" is the only story manuscript so dedicated, and perhaps Hemingway intended the dedication for Pauline's eyes only. Much about the abortion is left out of this deceptively simple "abortion story" (Baker 595)—not only the word itself, but also its metaphorical status in the context of the newlyweds' intimate history, and the dedication that provides the sign marked "To Biography." In its stead, Hemingway presents us with a narrative palimpsest, a structural and interpretive theme and variation.

The palimpsest of the published text, like much in the story itself—the white elephants, "Jig," the shadow of a cloud, "across," the smiles, the act of moving the suitcases, nearly every spoken pronoun (Josephs 55), and almost all the dialogue—can almost impossibly support two equal and opposite meanings. But no matter how we choose, each by each, to approach the story, to resolve these oppositions, the story is about much more than the end of a shallow relationship or the expedient operation necessary to keep it that way.

The reemergence of the themes and images of "Hills Like White Elephants" in *The Garden of Eden* (specifically, the gender-switching experiments in which David and Catherine indulge), and the manner with which Hemingway treated them in that later novel, supports and affirms the reading of "Hills" as based on cross-gendered autobiography. The highly charged images of suitcases, elephants, food, and fire from these early, paired stories all resurface in *Eden,* the story of a honeymoon set, at least initially, at Grau du Roi, where Hemingway wrote "Hills." In *The Garden of Eden,* begun approximately twenty years after Hemingway's own honeymoon, questions of betrayal and commitment reemerge in conjunction with these same symbols, but in the service of even the larger issue only hinted at in these early stories: writing, and its dangerous transformation of the private to create the public, as I will discuss in the next chapter. Although critics have long noted the autobiographical sources for the stories, and biographers have implied that Hemingway seemed to have a singularly undeveloped conscience when confronted with the choice between maintaining privacy and transforming his intimate life (and those of his acquaintances) into public property in his writing, none has explicitly addressed the act of writing as the site of this transformation and, consequently, as an act and site that would become, for Hemingway, "the Last Good Country" to which he ever strove to return. In other words, the act of transforming memory into text became, in itself, a place and a time for Hemingway.

Returning to this place and time became ever more difficult, because his increasing public acclaim as author and, later, icon interfered materially with the collection of fresh experiences to remember and transform into text. By the end of his life it was not his children who encumbered him, but the baggage of his multiple and conflicting identities, roles, and responsibilities, all of which he had eagerly courted. In other words, and at the risk of sounding tautological, his writing, once it became public, interfered with his writing. Being Hemingway, he would naturally address this experience in writing.

In 1927, however, domestic matters still dominated much of his thoughts and his writing. He had just left his first wife, Hadley, having publicly chronicled in his Personal fiction his unhappiness with the marriage and the intimate secrets of his betrayal of her with another woman, and having flirted with exposing his delight with his new bride with the publication of "Hills Like White Elephants." Despite this delight, and the heights of complexity to which it brought his writing, he would later claim to have loved Hadley "first and best" (quoted in Burwell 30). Between 1923 and 1929, Hemingway became the writer he would similarly claim to love the same way. This period was the last during which Hemingway the writer would own his own writing, and the next-to-last time he would own his own life. His hard-won freedom was, paradoxically, about to end.

CHAPTER THREE

THE NECESSARY DANGER

Writing *The Garden of Eden*

Know how complicated it is and then state it simply.
    —*The Garden of Eden*

Nothing of him that doth fade
But doth suffer a sea change
Into something rich and strange.
    —William Shakespeare, *The Tempest*

The *Garden of Eden*, in its published version,[1] is a novel about a honeymoon, haircuts, gender experimentation; a novel about Spain, France, sex, food, and drink; and, incidentally, a novel about a writer writing. In its manuscript version,[2] however, the honeymoon, hair, gender, sex, and drink form only one strand of another Hemingway double helix. The other strand concerns writing: as vocation, occupation, and profession, and as text and textuality. Like the marriage tale and Nick Adams story sequences, which comprised the double helix of Hemingway's early Personal writing, this later novel takes as its subject matter, its structure, and its central problem two strands of related ideas. Each of the thematic nuances present by implication in the doubled strands of the early Personal writing reemerge here, as do textual elements of the early stories themselves. But the novel takes a step back. *The Garden of Eden* manuscript not only extends this early double helix; it takes it as its central subject.

The double helix of Hemingway's early Personal fiction is both textual and thematic; by the time he began writing *The Garden of Eden,* he not only understood the latitudinal links (between paired stories and paired themes, given below in rows) but also the longitudinal ones (between the stories and thematic elements in each column).

Hemingway's Early Personal Fiction

Paired Stories

Marriage Tales	*Nick Adams Stories*
"Out of Season"	
"Cat in the Rain"	"The Doctor and the Doctor's Wife"
"Cross-Country Snow"	"The End of Something"/ "The Three-Day Blow"
"A Canary for One"	"In Another Country"/ "Now I Lay Me" [orig. "IAC II"]
"Hills Like White Elephants"	"Ten Indians"

Related Themes

Women with Men	Men without Women
Fertility	Virility
Creation	Transformation
Privacy	Publication
Intimacy	Exposure
Secrecy	Exhibitionism
Vocation	Profession
Writer	Author

For the mature Hemingway, questions of creation and transformation, of privacy and publication, of fertility and virility, and of writing and authorship were aspects of each other, as were his texts; like his texts, such questions were interdependent and mutually informative. There was but one question, ever. It was complicated but could be stated simply: whether or not to make public that which was private. The answer was equally simple, and equally complicated. The answer was the Text.

In Hemingway's early Personal fiction, the productive tension between these paired themes vitalized the writing of the paired stories. In *The Garden of Eden,* Hemingway tells the story of a writer, David Bourne, discovering the productivity of this tension within his own creative process as he lives and writes his honeymoon narrative (his marriage tale) while also writing stories of himself as a son (his own Nick Adams–like stories).

Hemingway's early creative process is his later subject matter. *The Garden of Eden* is the story not just of a writer's honeymoon but of the honeymoon's relationship to the writing. This relationship is complex, but it can be stated simply. In the novel, David comes to understand the objective similarities between his and Catherine's gender-role transformation (effected partially by haircutting and clipping) and his own multiple roles as writer and author (illustrated in part by his reading his own reviews, referred to as "cuttings" and "clippings"). Marita seems to understand these similarities instinctively. Catherine does not seem to understand them at all.

This is not all that Hemingway was doing in *The Garden of Eden*. He was also, in the unpublished "Andy" sections, considering his other mode of writing, the Authentic (as opposed to the Personal). He was thus additionally considering the difference he had begun to perceive in the late 1920s between a writer and an author (a difference effected through publication, which he had addressed in *Death in the Afternoon;* see chapter 4). More specifically, he was considering the effect of his authorship on his writing, and his abandonment of short story form in favor of the novels, which was at least partially a side effect of his desire for continued success as an author, and which had informed—or perhaps misinformed—his work in the 1930s.

While doing all this in *The Garden of Eden,* Hemingway was writing another Personal novel, *Islands in the Stream* (a father-son story that comprises the counterpart to *The Garden of Eden*'s marriage tale), and as work on both novels continued into the 1950s, he was pairing this pair of Personal novels with a pair of Authentic ones: *A Moveable Feast* and *True at First Light.* All these works specifically reference all his earlier ones—and the experiences that informed these early works, as well as his experiences since writing them. These experiences included reading *Tender Is the Night,* "The Bear," Dante's *Divine Comedy,* Proust's *Remembrance of Things Past,* and, arguably, Ibsen's *Hedda Gabler,* aspects of which *also* emerge in Hemingway's postwar fiction.

Anyone who has ever wondered why Hemingway had trouble finishing books in the postwar period need look no further. As he told interviewer Harvey Breit in 1950, "In writing I have moved through arithmetic, through plane geometry and algebra, and now I am in calculus. If they don't understand that, to hell with them" (Breit, "Talk").

Biographical and Creative Context

As Rose Marie Burwell argues in her extensive study of the manuscript and typescript drafts of the posthumous novels, Hemingway embarked after World War II on multiple simultaneous projects that would occupy him for the rest of his writing life. The first of these projects was a novel, begun in 1946, that he would almost immediately split into two (Burwell 1).[3] Portions of these narratives would later be published as *Islands in the Stream* and *The Garden of Eden*. *Islands in the Stream* concerns the life, work, and relationships of a divorced painter, Thomas Hudson, especially his relationships with his three sons. As in *Islands*'s 1920s counterparts, the Nick Adams stories, the affective power of father-son relationships drives this later novel.

The Garden of Eden, as edited by Tom Jenks, concerns the writer David Bourne and his rich wife Catherine on their honeymoon and is set in the late 1920s, primarily in the same Provençal and Spanish towns that the writer Hemingway visited in 1927 with his new, wealthy wife Pauline Pfeiffer. In its unpublished form, however, *The Garden of Eden* clearly reveals Hemingway's postwar return to Personal writing and to the intertextual creative process that had produced some of his best early fiction. The paired stories of the 1920s reemerge in *The Garden of Eden* (contextually, textually, structurally, and thematically). Together, the postwar Personal novels reflect Hemingway's return to the productive tension of linked pairs, one element of which concerns fertility (women with men), the other virility (men without women, but thinking about them, in the company of other men, especially in father-son relationships). Together, the late novels continue to address the problems of the artist: the questions of creativity, writing, and authorship, all of which emerged in Hemingway's work in the late 1920s, and to which he shifted his attention in the 1930s, largely abandoning his Personal fiction in favor of Authentic writing (*Death in the Afternoon, Green Hills of Africa,* and *The Fifth Column*), and the short story in favor of book-length works.

The Garden of Eden, however, does much more than *reflect* these paired issues; it *represents* them as central to its plot. It is more than an element of what Burwell calls Hemingway's "portrait of the artist" (1); it is Hemingway's textual autobiography. Here he writes the story of the writer writing, as well as the story of the stories that writer writes. Reconstructing Hemingway's creative process from the 1920s reveals that David Bourne's creative process in *The Garden of Eden* is Hemingway's. Identifying Hemingway's Personal fiction from the 1920s as a double helix of linked trajectories (marriage-fertility tales and Nick Adams–virility tales) confirms that David Bourne's honeymoon narrative and Africa stories comprise Bourne's creative double helix and affirms the critical value of considering Hemingway's texts as contextually autobiographical.

Of the Africa stories, the one whose composition is most fully represented in *The Garden of Eden* is the elephant story. The central image that will become the elephant story occurs to David as he tries to shake off remorse after a night of gender switching with Catherine by taking a long walk around Madrid (just as the abortion idea occurred to Hemingway in his letters to Pauline, seven months before he wrote "Hills Like White Elephants"): "But use your head for what it is worth. I do, he told himself. I have but in this it is only the needle on the compass. I know the direction but there are no maps and it is a new country. It's new only to us of course. No countries are new. Yes they are. They are new to everyone who comes to them for the first time. And all new countries[4] are forbidden by something. So where do you go? I don't know. And what will you find? I don't know. The bones of the others I suppose" (KL/EH 422.1/8, 10).

While contemplating his marriage, then, David metaphorizes it as a new country, one to which he has no map.[5] Soon he will write about Africa when it was new to him, when he was young and had no idea how the story would end (similar to having no map and not knowing what he would find). What he will find are the bones of a dead elephant, which ultimately trap the live one he has seen by moonlight. Hemingway's depiction of the origin of the bones idea, and of David's psyche and creative process, is very subtle. As David thinks about Catherine, the phrase "the bones of the others" comes to him with no explanation, no fanfare. One month later, and a few days after Catherine has (after a month of being a girl) again switched genders in the bedroom, he begins to write the elephant bones story:

> He left the narrative [the narrative about his and Catherine's honeymoon] where he was to write a story that had come to him four or five days before [when Catherine had again switched genders in the bedroom] and had been developing, he thought, in the last two nights when he had slept so well. He knew it was bad to interrupt any work he was engaged in but he felt confident and sure. . . .
>
> . . . It was a good story and now, remembering he remembered how long he had intended to write it. The story had not come to him in the past few days. His memory had been inaccurate in that. It was the necessity to write it that had come to him. He knew how the story ended now. (KL/EH 422.1/14, 1–2)

At first, it seems that Catherine's most recent switching triggers this story; but David then remembers that no, it had come earlier (in Madrid, after another switch). In this passage David remembers remembering[6]; David, now in France, remembers beginning to remember, in Madrid, the elephant episode from his childhood. Why he remembers the elephant episode when he does is crucial. He has begun to realize that both Catherine and the elephant have been betrayed by their natures, Catherine in her growing madness and the elephant in continuing to visit the bones of his dead companion, which renders him easy to track and results in his death. David is not yet consciously aware of Catherine's madness. In his own use of *remate,* he is rebounding his present off his past. He has begun to appreciate the similarities between his current situation and the story he writes of his past, but if he senses how his and Catherine's story will end, it is still, at this point in the novel, subconsciously. Both stories end in betrayal: in one, David comes to feel that he has betrayed the elephant by telling his father about it and then chooses to betray his father by silently disagreeing with him regarding the rectitude of his feelings; in the other, David realizes that long before Catherine betrays him, he has betrayed Catherine—not exactly by abandoning the honeymoon narrative, as she believes, but by silently deciding not to publish it, as she so avidly desires. As with so much else in Hemingway, all this can only be realized retrospectively. I will give a detailed account of why David makes this decision, although it is never stated in the novel, in the Andy section; for now, my point is that David considers the honeymoon narrative merely Authentic. He chooses not to betray his writing; in so doing, he betrays—and passes judgment on—his wife.

Contextual inquiry into David's text requires that the text be understood within a larger context: Hemingway's own. The text of *The Garden of Eden* depends to a great extent on its own context. Although Burwell has established the thematic links among Hemingway's postwar tetralogy, she does not consider either their status as chronological end points in lifelong, career-spanning thematic and textual trajectories, or the extent to which they inform Hemingway's earlier works (or vice versa). Considering *The Garden of Eden* as one of these end points, and identifying in it concerns that have not yet seen representation in the Personal fiction (Personal versus Authentic, short story versus novel, and writer versus author), reveals that in addition to referencing and explicating Hemingway's early Personal fiction, it also addresses centrally the concerns within—and surrounding—*Death in the Afternoon* (written 1930–1932), the book that (temporarily) destroyed Hemingway's critical reputation, as I will discuss at length in chapter 4.

Hemingway's life in the years immediately following World War II resonated with his France years, especially 1925–1928. Because the story of *The Garden of Eden* was not only a product but also a representation of specific creative and professional concerns, I will address how those concerns emerge in the context of the novel (and the writing of the novel) after I discuss how situations in Hemingway's Personal and domestic life in the mid-1940s triggered memories of, and focused his thinking on, Paris and Provence in 1925–1928.

After World War II, Hemingway was strongly reminded of two of the central figures from his France years, Pauline Pfeiffer and F. Scott Fitzgerald. Although Hemingway and Pauline had divorced in 1940 (their marriage broke down a few years earlier, when Hemingway began his very public affair with Martha Gellhorn, who became, briefly, his third wife), the spring of 1946 forced a lengthy (and probably platonic) reunion. That spring, their son Patrick developed a serious illness while staying at the Finca Vigía with Hemingway and his fourth wife, Mary. Mary, however, was called to Chicago to minister to her father, who had just been diagnosed with cancer. Pauline came to Cuba to nurse Patrick and stayed through the summer, moving into the guest house after Mary returned from the States.

Whether or not the three lived in physical intimacy as an active ménage à trois is irrelevant; what matters is that the situation at the Finca was similar to an earlier one, when Pauline had briefly lived and traveled with Ernest and Hadley in the 1920s. Having Pauline at the Finca with himself and Mary doubtless evoked Hemingway's memories of 1925–1926; both the mid-1920s and the mid-1940s, then, informed the Catherine-David-Marita arrangement (and its unrealized counterpart, Nick-Barbara-Andy) in *The Garden of Eden*.

Pauline's association with Hemingway was, first, personal—she had been his lover and wife and was the mother of his younger sons Patrick and Gregory—but it was also creative and professional. Creatively, she was intimately linked to the Personal fiction from both the 1926 dark period, during which Ernest was separated both from her and from Hadley and was uncertain as to their futures, and from their 1927 honeymoon, when Hemingway represented their recent history in the cross-gendered autobiographical "Hills Like White Elephants" (see chapter 2).

Pauline's influence on Hemingway's writing after 1925 cannot be overestimated. His 1926 separation from and 1927 reunion with her contributed directly to much of the best fiction in *Men Without Women;* her first pregnancy coincided with Catherine's in *A Farewell to Arms;* and her wealth made possible the critically risky *Death in the Afternoon* and the safari that resulted in the poorly received *Green Hills of Africa*. When their relationship started to sour, aspects of Pauline (and of Zelda Fitzgerald and Jane Mason) began to emerge in Hemingway's fictional depictions of the rich wives who proved dangerous to their husbands (in, for example, "The Snows of Kilimanjaro" and "The Short Happy Life of Francis Macomber," the last of Hemingway's short fiction to appear in collection in his lifetime, and arguably some of his best). Pauline also figured prominently, although invisibly, in *For Whom the Bell Tolls*. The character Pilar was named after Hemingway's boat; however, the boat was named after Pauline—Pilar was one of Ernest's early nicknames for her (Eby 44) and was the name they planned to give the daughter they never had (Reynolds, *Homecoming* 169).

Professionally, their mutual decision to return to the United States for the birth of their first child brought Hemingway's fame home to him in a way that living in a French-speaking country never had. Right around the time of his divorce, and because of "rumors that had arisen about his early life," he asked Scribner's to "lay off the Biography" in their promotional materials (quoted in Trogdon 100), doubtless in an attempt to preserve some privacy for himself, his growing family, and his writing. Finally, Pauline's family money provided him the necessary safety net to accept the risk of writing *Death in the Afternoon* (Reynolds, *1930s* 41), in which the problems of professional writing, authorship, and the business of art comprise a central concern, and with the money for the 1933–1934 safari he chronicled in *Green Hills of Africa*. Hemingway's critical reputation, shaky after *Death in the Afternoon*, suffered even more after *Green Hills of Africa*.

By the early 1930s, Pauline's uncle, Gus Pfeiffer, had helped finance a $50,000 trust fund for Ernest's mother, bought him a house, and sent him to Africa (Reynolds, *Chronology* 57, 64, 69, 72). How logical a cause and effect line there may be between Pauline's money and the critical censure Hemingway experienced in the 1930s is questionable; but if his fiction in the late 1930s is any indication, Hemingway, at least, drew that line clearly.

By 1946, though, the personal, professional, and fiscal issues surrounding Hemingway's second marriage were resolved. Since 1940, when that marriage ended and he sold the movie rights to *For Whom the Bell Tolls*, Hemingway had been supporting himself and his extended family, without any assistance from his wives' trust funds or families, for the first time in his life (Trogdon 4). He was ready for the return of the woman who was ever his best muse, who would return him by association to the site of some of his best early writing.

F. Scott Fitzgerald's association with Hemingway was the inverse of Pauline's. He was first a professional contact, then a collaborator and competitor in creativity, and finally a personal friend. Although Fitzgerald had died in 1940, his first biographers began to contact Hemingway after the war, asking him to share his memories of the writer who had been, early on, his professional mentor and, for a while longer, his friend.[7] His friendship with Fitzgerald had long ago suffered, especially after his negative response to Fitzgerald's last published novel, *Tender Is the Night* (1934). Hemingway's disgust at Zelda Fitzgerald's effect on her husband's writing (and Scott's unwillingness to resist this effect) had increased throughout the 1930s; by 1940, when Fitzgerald died, Hemingway had given up hope that Fitzgerald would ever regain his early excellence as a writer.

Remembering Fitzgerald reminded Hemingway of his years in France, especially the south of France in the late 1920s. By then, both writers had published two novels (like David Bourne in *The Garden of Eden,* also set in Provence and the Riviera during the same period). They enjoyed roughly equal stature based on the critical reception of Fitzgerald's *This Side of Paradise* (1920) and *The Great Gatsby* (1925) and Hemingway's *The Sun Also Rises* (1926) and *A Farewell to Arms* (1929). At least three of these novels (*The Great Gatsby,*[8] *The Sun Also Rises,* and *A Farewell to Arms*) contributed to Hemingway's *The Garden of Eden* (I will discuss their specific contributions in a later section); in the context of his relationship with Fitzgerald, however, a later novel, *Tender Is the Night,* would contribute even more strongly.[9]

In "Hemingway's Barbershop Quintet: *The Garden of Eden* Manuscript," Mark Spilka argues that Hemingway's "standoff with Fitzgerald" led him to colonize Fitzgerald's *Tender Is the Night* in *The Garden of Eden,* borrowing freely from its structure, plot, and composite characters (354). Spilka's chief contention is that, like Fitzgerald in *Tender Is the Night,* Hemingway displaced his psychosexual insecurities onto the act of writing in *The Garden of Eden.* Based on this contention, Spilka concludes that "the novel is chiefly about hair cuts" (354). An understanding of the status of the *Garden of Eden* manuscript within Hemingway's overall Personal text, however, indicates that Spilka's contention is backward—and thus that his conclusion elides half of Hemingway's project.

Spilka locates in both writers similar psychosexual anxieties (he identifies these as androgyny),[10] which, he contends, they both projected into their very similar novels. Spilka's purpose is, in part, to counter Angus Collins's argument in "Homosexuality and the Genesis of *Tender Is the Night*" that "certain homosexual sequences in 'The World's Fair,' an early version of *Tender Is the Night,* are 'projections of vocational insecurity'" (Spilka 352). Spilka insists that the problem confronting both Hemingway and Fitzgerald was not homosexuality, as Collins argues, but androgyny (thus glossing over Collins's second term, "vocation"). Spilka asserts that Hemingway, in *The Garden of Eden,* "would confront the hazards of androgyny that Fitzgerald . . . had only dimly understood, and would overcome them through courageous masculine artistry" (353). This contribution to "the manly man versus the effete Princetonian debate," which has long since worn out its critical usefulness, is irrelevant. Whatever Fitzgerald may have been doing, Collins's teleological conclusion is apt for Hemingway—that he was projecting vocational (and professional) anxieties onto scenes of sexual confusion in his novel. He was not merely using his novel to come to terms with psychosexual issues. Spilka, in any case, is comparing David Bourne, Hemingway's character, to Fitzgerald. In *The Garden of Eden,* the one who begins to understand the links between sex games and subject matter is *David.* Even if David Bourne is a representation of Hemingway, he is but a very early Hemingway—the Hemingway of 1927 or so. At the very least, Spilka's desire to attribute the anxieties of a twenty-seven-year-old to a forty-seven-year-old strips the older Hemingway of perspective—on himself, and on Fitzgerald's novel.

Moreover, for Spilka to suggest that Hemingway's early tonsorial experimentation and androgynous tendencies were a later anxiety seems disingenuous. Far from keeping secret his interest in hair as an object of sexual arousal, Hemingway had gone public with it—personally, in portraiture (the Waldo Pierce portrait)[11] and in print[12]—as early as the 1920s. He may have performed anxiety in the company of his male friends (e.g., lying about his suddenly red hair, saying he'd thought Mary's hair dye was shampoo), but his lifelong interest in the sexual possibilities of hair as the site at which to blur gender lines and the frequency with which such scenes appeared in his fiction suggest that by 1946, long familiarity with himself as a sexual being might have reduced his anxiety level somewhat.

A writer's vocation is to write, but his profession is to publish, to be an author. Authorship carries with it a different anxiety, one that was at least as important to both Hemingway and Fitzgerald in their respective times as any underlying concerns about psychosexuality: the problem of being compelled to publish that which might best be left private, a compulsion Hemingway had addressed as early as "A Canary for One." This compulsion was a central issue for the writer of *Tender Is the Night* and in the text of *The Garden of Eden.* In writing *Tender Is the Night,* Fitzgerald was exploiting Zelda's mental illness (especially if, as Nancy Comley argues, several of Nicole's sanitarium letters to Dick were actual letters from Zelda to Scott). In writing *The Garden of Eden,* Hemingway was remembering having exploited his early marital problems in his Personal fiction, and inverting it. David's reluctance to publish the honeymoon narrative indicates a reticence that Hemingway of the 1920s did not feel, but one that he did feel later, in the early 1930s. What Spilka interprets as an anxiety may, at least for Hemingway in the early 1930s, be nothing more than retrospective embarrassment—the embarrassment of an older person at his younger behavior (however anxiety ridden it may have been then), the embarrassment of a newly public figure at his behavior from a time when he was less well known. In the 1930s, Hemingway had cut his hair short and left it that way; he had also abandoned his Personal writing in favor of the Authentic.

Pauline's presence as a third at the Finca, combined with Hemingway's relatively new financial freedom, sparked a return to his Personal writing, which he had largely abandoned in 1929, when increasing media interest in his Personal life had increased his own desire for privacy and had drawn attention away from his writing. That he had courted this attention, and continued to court it even after its danger (to his writing) became apparent, was a conflict that he never resolved. Nor could he. For him, this was the writer-author paradox (see chapter 4).

What is implicit in Spilka's debate with Collins is that both Hemingway and Fitzgerald displaced sexual insecurities onto their vocation. In Hemingway's case, reversing this displacement (and being chronologically flexible) may be more useful: the later Hemingway displaced his early vocational and professional concerns onto scenes of sexual ambiguity in his later fiction. Unlike Fitzgerald, the older Hemingway had had time to appreciate what he had suspected since 1929—that vocation was but one aspect of literary creativity, the others being occupation, profession, and authorship (see chapter 4). Hemingway had tried to warn Fitzgerald of the implicit hazards in forgetting this fact, specifically in reference to *Tender Is the Night*.

Hemingway's initial response to *Tender Is the Night* was negative. He first expressed this in a letter dated April 30, 1934, to their mutual editor, Maxwell Perkins:

> In spite of marvellous [*sic*] places there is something wrong with it and, as a writer, this is what I believe is wrong. He starts with two people, Gerald and Sara Murphy. . . .
>
> But anyway he takes a strong woman like Sara . . . and first arbitrarily makes her into a psychopathic case and then makes her into Zelda, then back into Sara, finally into nothing. It's bloody hopeless.
>
> Gerald is Gerald for a while, then made-up, the made-up part is good, then becomes Scott and has things happen to him that could

never happen to Gerald. . . . So you are never convinced. (quoted in Bruccoli, *Friendship* 166)

Although Hemingway appears to object to the psychological inconsistency of creating composite characters, he had done something similar in nearly all his Personal writing (and would do nearly the same thing to all the same people, and more, in *The Garden of Eden*). He later wrote to Fitzgerald, "Goddamn it you took liberties with peoples pasts and futures that produced not people but damned marvellously [*sic*] faked case histories" (quoted in Bruccoli, *Friendship* 171). Either Fitzgerald's characters are inconsistent, as Hemingway implied to Perkins, or they are consistent but unreal, as he told Fitzgerald. Or perhaps something else was bothering him.

This something else was authorship and its attendant pressures, as he implies in a later section of the same letter: "For Christ sake write and don't worry about what the boys will say . . . you can't think well enough to sit down and write a deliberate masterpiece and if you could get rid of Seldes and those guys that nearly ruined you and turn them out as well as you can and let the spectators yell when it is good and hoot when it is not you would be all right" (quoted in Bruccoli, *Friendship* 172). The connections in Hemingway's mind between basing characters on real people and feeling anxious about critical attention was not incidental. He had long made a practice of the first and had become embittered by the second, specifically by those critics (in this context, reviewers) who focused more on the reality behind the writing than on the writing itself. As he complained to Max Perkins in a November 17, 1933, letter, "If I write about anybody—automatically they label the character as me . . . What shit. . . . Nobody can tell which ones I make up completely" (quoted in Bruccoli and Trogdon 202).

And the connections went deeper. At this time, Gertrude Stein's *The Autobiography of Alice B. Toklas* was appearing serially, and her depiction of Hemingway was not flattering, especially in its guise as nonfiction. Hemingway may also have objected to the similarity between himself (the persona he had affected, the public image he had courted) and Fitzgerald's character Tommy Barban, the French mercenary for whom Nicole Diver leaves her husband Dick.[13] Tommy's boast to Nicole as they embrace on the beach seems to have been lifted straight from Hemingway's mouth (and pen): "'After all, I am a hero,' Tommy said calmly, only half joking. 'I have ferocious courage, usually, something like a lion, something like a drunken man'" (*Tender* 270). Bruccoli notes that Fitzgerald "made warning notes to himself in the manuscript" to "beware Ernest" and "avoid Hemingway" and asserts (probably rightly) that Fitzgerald was trying to avoid Hemingway's style (*Friendship* 162). However, the latter warning occurs in a section about Tommy Costello (later Tommy Barban; see reproduction of manuscript, also on 162). Fitzgerald was also probably trying to avoid putting too much of Hemingway's person into the Tommy character.

For these reasons, the danger about which Hemingway was trying to warn Fitzgerald in his response to *Tender Is the Night* was the danger of being unable to control perceptions of one's public self. Dick Diver's professional and personal failure in the novel was too revealing of Scott's own—and too much what Hemingway feared—to risk exposing it in public.

By 1933, Hemingway had already announced his judgment (in *Death in the Afternoon*) that the publicity attendant on authorship was bad for writing; nothing he learned between then and 1946 caused him to alter that judgment. In *The Garden of Eden,* though, his project was somewhat different from Fitzgerald's thirteen years before. Although he too relied on composite characters (blurring Pauline, Martha, Jane, and Zelda, at least, in the character of Catherine) and made them do things their real-life counterparts never would have done, the mature Hemingway was representing a moment in his past, not his present. In that past moment, he had hardly had time to identify his own anxieties (whether psychosexual or vocational and professional), much less to understand that all of them involved in some way the problem of publication—of making public.

The Garden of Eden shows that by 1946 he understood that publication was common to his early anxieties, and that that very commonality might make a very interesting novel. Catherine's exhibitionism requires the publication (both in haircuts and in print) of the androgynous eros in her marriage; David is caught between his love for his wife and her desire to publish what he feels should be private. Catherine seems compelled to broadcast their bedroom secrets, their gender switching, first by telling Nick and Barbara, then the Colonel, then Marita, and then by assuming the fantasy role of "very great publisher" (KL/EH 422.1/28, 47) of the honeymoon narrative (which David has by this time stopped writing, for many reasons, including not wanting to publish the account of Catherine's growing madness). Moreover, David is also caught between his desire to write well, which for him means writing his Personal short fiction, and pressure from Catherine, his self-styled publisher, and perhaps from his real one, to publish another book. After he abandons the honeymoon narrative to work on the Africa stories, there is no book in the offing.

David's dilemma reflects Hemingway's own from the 1930s. Letters between Hemingway and Max Perkins concerning *For Whom the Bell Tolls* tacitly reflect the decline in Hemingway's reputation after *his* second novel in 1929. When Hemingway suggested delaying *For Whom the Bell Tolls* and putting out a book of stories first, Perkins gently dissuaded him. As Trogdon suggests, "Perkins seems to have understood that what Hemingway needed to publish to save his reputation was a real novel, not a short story collection or a novel made by fusing together a group of short stories as was the case of *To Have and Have Not*" (385). He continues, "For most of the critics, *For Whom the Bell Tolls* was the novel they had been waiting for since *A Farewell to Arms*" (423): Edmund Wilson announced "Hemingway the artist is with us again, and it is like having an old friend back" (quoted in Trogdon 422), and Lionel Trilling remarked that "here, we feel at once, is a restored Hemingway writing to the top of his bent" (quoted in Trogdon 423).

Spilka's assertion that "*The Garden of Eden,* in its roughly completed manuscript form, is chiefly a novel about haircuts" ("Barbershop" 353) errs primarily in its adverb. Especially "in its roughly completed manuscript form," textually and contextually, it is chiefly a novel about publishing and writing, specifically about the writing of the paired stories it represents: both the story of David and Catherine's honeymoon (in which the haircutting is a chief concern) and the story of David writing while on that honeymoon. David and Catherine's honeymoon and David writing form the double helix of *The Garden of Eden* in the same manner that the honeymoon narrative and the Africa stories form the double helix of David's writing within the novel—just as stories of fertility and virility, of marriage and father-son relationships, of women with men and men without women formed the double helix of Hemingway's early Personal writing. In 1946, his problem, or, less pathologically, his interest, was in the interstices between context and text, wherein he decided what to write, and between writing as a vocation and as a profession, wherein he decided what to publish.

The climactic moment in *The Garden of Eden* concerns not a haircut, but rather Catherine Bourne's burning of her husband's Africa stories (of which there were only single copies, the first drafts). Two questions drive the plot: Will David cut his hair to match Catherine's? (which by the burning scene he has already done, twice, and, although he is made uncomfortable by how much he enjoys it, he admits to himself that he does); and also, Will David be able to write? This question is asked and answered, in the affirmative, three times: after the first haircut, after the second, and after Catherine burns the manuscripts of his Africa stories.[14]

Catherine burns only one of the two sets of stories that David has written. Like Hemingway, David also writes marriage and father-son stories simultaneously, two at a time: the long honeymoon narrative, which is the nonfiction marriage tale (and, as such, was for David "authentic," as I will discuss in the Andy section), and three short stories about his boyhood and his father (the Africa story sequence, which for David was "personal").

David's stories are the fictional counterparts of Hemingway's early paired stories, especially (but not exclusively) those he wrote on his own 1927 honeymoon, the marriage tale "Hills Like White Elephants" and the father-son story "Ten Indians." These stories, along with "The Sea Change," "A Canary for One," "In Another Country," "Now I Lay Me," "Cross-Country Snow," "The Three-Day Blow," "Cat in the Rain," and "The Doctor and the Doctor's Wife" (see chapters 1 and 2), and the books *A Farewell to Arms, The Sun Also Rises,* and—somewhat surprisingly—*Death in the Afternoon* all comprise early versions of what became, in various ways, *The Garden of Eden.*

Text

The hundreds of references to, and quotations of, Hemingway's early fiction, his early creative process, and *Death in the Afternoon* in *The Garden of Eden* tend to cluster around moments of extreme psychosexual tension and the tension between creativity and professional writing. Both kinds of tension hinge, more broadly, on questions of publication. Earlier works and issues that inform *The Garden of Eden* are, specifically:

1. The two stories that Hemingway wrote and/or completed while on his Grau du Roi honeymoon in May 1927 (where *The Garden of Eden* opens): "Hills Like White Elephants" and "Ten Indians" (the honeymoon fiction);
2. "The Sea Change," which seems to fit neatly into the novel's plot (though it was written fifteen years before);
3. several early works concerning questions of fertility and virility, which inform two of Catherine and David's arguments about fertility (in which several of the early stories figure prominently), the second of which leads directly to questions of writing and authorship;
4. the Personal versus Authentic writing tension, which manifests in the Andy section, suggesting an explanation for David's decision not to publish the honeymoon narrative even before he realizes the extent of Catherine's illness; and
5. *Death in the Afternoon,* both in the fact of its existence and in its text (including excised material).

"Hills Like White Elephants" and "Ten Indians"

In the opening pages of *The Garden of Eden,* "David wished that he had brought a casting rod and spoons so that he might cast out across the flow of water" (KL/EH 422.1/1, 6). The term "spoons" is somewhat arcane; it refers to a bright, concave metal disk around which fish hooks are attached. Another term for such a device, both lure and hook, is "jig." As I discussed in the previous chapter, Jig is the name of the young pregnant woman in "Hills Like White Elephants" who acts as a bright lure with potentially dangerous hooks for the man who has fathered her child. Catherine is another one of these hooked lures. As the beautiful and damned heroine of *The Garden of Eden,* she will lure David into erotic gender-switching adventures that will both shame and excite him until he understands them. After the first of these adventures, David, like the American man in "Hills Like White Elephants," knows only that their previous life is over: "He held her close and hard and inside himself he said goodbye and then goodbye and goodbye" (KL/EH 422.1/1, 27).

The concurrence of the writing of "Hills Like White Elephants" and "Ten Indians" illuminates a highly personal linkage between honeymoons and the theme of fatherhood, between romantic commitment and paternal betrayal. When considered in light of the story of Hadley, the lost valise of manuscripts, and her subsequent pregnancy, these two stories come to evince a complex personal semiotic of love and fatherhood involving, of all things, suitcases and elephants (both of which connect to the possibilities of romantic and paternal commitment in "Hills Like White Elephants") and food (which serves as the nourishing counterpoint to romantic and paternal betrayal in "Ten Indians").

Hemingway's 1927 honeymoon formally celebrated his union and reunion with the woman he considered "the same person" as himself (KL/EH Correspondence, 1926), and whose possibly indefinite separation from him had felt, as he told her in a letter, like "an abortion" (*SL* 234). "Hills Like White Elephants" is (perhaps) the first moment in Hemingway's fiction where he explores the possibility of cross-gendered autobiographical representation. In *The Garden of Eden,* David and Catherine's first cross-gendered erotic encounter occurs in Grau du Roi. There, Catherine turns herself into a boy and David into a girl, just as Hemingway had done, writing "Hills Like White Elephants" there twenty years before—when he had turned himself into Jig and Pauline into the American man.

Several other elements of "Hills Like White Elephants" are transformed in *The Garden of Eden,* not the least of which are elephants and suitcases.

The suitcases represents the resolution to the white elephant problem of the abortion; at least in the writerly text, when the man moves the suitcases, he agrees to fatherhood and thus turns his back on the romantic and paternal betrayal he had advocated earlier in the story. The suitcases and elephants re-emerge in the later novel in conjunction with elements from the other story from Hemingway's 1927 honeymoon, "Ten Indians."

"Ten Indians" also dramatizes romantic and paternal betrayal. Nick Adams learns that his Native American girlfriend, Prudie, has betrayed him; the bringer of these bad tidings is his father. In an early draft of this story, Dr. Adams feels he has betrayed his son by telling him; all he has been able to give him by way of comfort is food. This draft was written in a *cahier,* similar to those in which David Bourne writes his Nick Adams–like stories in *The Garden of Eden.*

Here questions of betrayal and commitment reemerge in conjunction with these same narrative elements: food shared by David and Catherine is posited in counterpoint to her later betrayals of him; these betrayals involve infidelity (when she sleeps with Marita) and her taking his *cahiers* out of his suitcase to burn them. One of the stories she burns concerns a younger David with his African fiancée (a cognate for Nick's Native American girlfriend Prudie). Another story is the elephant story, also set in Africa (a cognate for Nick's Michigan), in which he betrays an elephant by revealing its presence to his father and to Juma, a hunter and their guide, echoing young Nick's "I know where there's black squirrels, Daddy" in "The Doctor and the Doctor's Wife" (76). David's "I know where there's an elephant, Daddy," though, triggers a darker ending.

David and Nick are both using these animals as a way to avoid the neurotic, intrusive female presence in their lives. Nick is escaping his mother, who is represented in "The Doctor and the Doctor's Wife" as a passive-aggressive hypochondriac. David, in writing the stories, manages briefly to escape his wife, Catherine. Although at this point she respects his need for privacy to work, she is slowly going crazy. Neither escape is successful. Nick's walk into the woods with his father provides only a temporary respite; David so strongly identifies the elephant with his wife that the more he writes, the closer she gets.

Young David, Juma, and his father track and kill the elephant, but along the way, David's father has taught him not to betray his own feelings. David comes to identify very strongly with the elephant when he learns that it continues to visit the bones of its dead friend, whom Juma had also killed; his father very clearly indicates that such sentiment is childish. This is a coming-of-age story in which David learns to protect things—the elephant and his own feelings—through silence, through choosing not to publish. By committing to himself, he betrays his father.

Hemingway, too, is like the elephant, revisiting the bones of "Hills Like White Elephants" and his other early stories, working on them a sea change, building them into the coral of his Mediterranean novel. The sea change he works on "Hills Like White Elephants" again involves a switching of genders; in its new version, meanings are reversed. In "Hills Like White Elephants," the man, after forcing Jig to agree to abort her pregnancy, changes his mind, accepts the third in their relationship, and makes the weighty commitment to fatherhood as he carries the two "heavy" (full) suitcases to the other side of the station. In *The Garden of Eden,* Catherine, the woman, upon discovering that she is not pregnant, empties David's suitcase of its father-son contents and burns them, trying to force him to abort his Africa stories to focus on their relationship. Whether or not she has succeeded in forcing this abortion is the question that, as in "Hills Like White Elephants," governs much of the remainder of the story.

"The Sea Change"

Another of Hemingway's early stories, "The Sea Change" (1930–1931) provided a particularly important point of return for *The Garden of Eden.* Paul Smith identifies the story as a source for the novel. He predicts that

> critics will inevitably consider this story as an early version of David Bourne's discovery of his wife's bisexuality and their later transsexual exercises (chap. 11 ff.). At the end of that chapter David ostensibly leaves for Paris when Catherine leaves his bed for Marita's; although he returns in the following chapter from Cannes, one can imagine the story's conversation in the Paris bar forming an epilogue to Catherine's confession of bisexuality. The similarity between the story and this part of the novel lends support to Robert Fleming's claim that Phil, in that story, is a writer like David Bourne—and, one would add, like Hubert Elliot who, somewhat more passively, suffers the same revelation in "Mr. and Mrs. Elliot" of April 1924. (*Guide* 226)

Although a number of critics (most notably Burwell, Eby, Comley and Scholes, and Spilka) note similarities among Hemingway's works, Smith's identification of "The Sea Change" as a "version" of *The Garden of Eden* is particularly evocative. He uses the term "version" to relate similar plot elements, yet as a textual scholar, he cannot have been blind to the textual implications of other, even stronger, shared details, which suggests that the word "version" may be even more apt than he implies in this brief paragraph.

Smith stops short of saying that "The Sea Change" was, in a way, a draft of *The Garden of Eden,* but his employment of the later novel as interpretive evidence for the earlier story is nearly a unique move in Hemingway criticism. Obviously, a later draft, or version, of a discrete text can be used to understand an earlier one. However, textual criticism generally works the other way—using early and later drafts to understand a singly titled published work. *The Garden of Eden* and "The Sea Change" (and several other earlier Hemingway works), although authorially published under different titles, are writerly versions of each other, as Smith's critical move implies.

"The Sea Change" contributes more to *The Garden of Eden* than Smith suggests. Phil, the name of its protagonist, was one of Hemingway's original names for David Bourne (KL/EH 422.1/1, 8). The story's title comes from Ariel's song in Shakespeare's *The Tempest,* elements of which emerge throughout *The Garden of Eden:*

Full fathom five thy father lies.
Of his bones are coral made.
Those are pearls that were his eyes.
Nothing of him that doth fade
But doth suffer a sea change
Into something rich and strange.
Sea nymphs hourly ring his knell. (1.2.397–403)[15]

Catherine and David both dye their hair to match her pearls (also a reminder of Sara Murphy, perhaps via *Tender Is the Night;* Sara was famous for wearing her long strand of pearls to the beach).[16] And as the sun bleaches their hair even lighter, as their hair "fades," David fears that his masculinity will likewise fade; he is changing, at Catherine's request, into Catherine (she calls him "Catherine" in bed, when she is "Peter"). Catherine, the sea nymph from the swimming scenes, is nothing if not rich and strange. In burning the manuscripts about David's father, she believes that she is ringing his father's knell. In writing the stories about his deceased father, David works his own sea change on his present, refracting it through his past: "You must write each day better than you possibly can and use the sorrow you have now to make you know how the early sorrow came" (KL/EH 422.1/23, 9). In rewriting the stories after Catherine has burned them, and thus resurrecting his father, he proves that her song—like Ariel's—is a lie.

Virility and Fertility

The Garden of Eden references the early stories in service to questions of fertility and virility. These references are so frequent that *The Garden of Eden* proposes a reconsideration of the early marriage tales and Nick Adams stories as fertility tales and virility tales, respectively, and suggests expanding these categories to include *A Farewell to Arms* (an obvious fertility tale) and *The Sun Also Rises* (an equally obvious virility tale). Hemingway's paired concepts (virility and fertility, writer and author, Personal and Authentic) often evince apparent synonymy. Under textual scrutiny, this synonymy dissolves,[17] resolving instead into a tightly linked pair. The tension between these pairs drives his best writing.

Fertility can technically relate to either men or women. Hemingway seems to have understood it as a private matter, a secret, internal thing. Virility, however, is in all its connotations male, and something that becomes public either by male performance of maleness (as in the Nick Adams stories) or by a woman's pregnancy (the intersection of the marriage tales and the Nick Adams stories in "Cross-Country Snow" when Helen is pregnant seems to confirm this). In Hemingway's understanding, virility works a transformation on fertility; fertility creates, and virility publicizes that creation.

All David's and Catherine's physical changes are visible in the mirror that Catherine purchases to put behind the bar in their lodgings, another point of contiguity with "The Sea Change." In that story, the abandoned man—also tan, also blond—tells the barman, "I'm a different man, James," and continues, "Vice . . . is a very strange thing." The young man looks at the woman, then, "as he looked in the glass, he saw he was really quite a different-looking man" (305). Looking in the mirror to confirm something about one's gender or sexuality is a device Hemingway used frequently.[18] David, after he has his hair dyed, looks into the full-length mirror and sees "really quite a different-looking man." He, like Phil, does not know himself at first; he is wondering, apparently, if he is still a man. What he sees initially puts him off:

> "Hello you son of a bitch," he said to the reflection. "I don't think I know you."
> "No?" the reflection looked back at him.

. . . His hair was cut like Catherine's and he was as blonde as the girl in Biarritz. (KL/EH 422.1/12, insert to 11)

However, remembering the girl in Biarritz gives him an erection:

> He remembered her and how she looked and how she had made him feel and he looked down and saw that thinking about her made him feel the same way again. He looked at the mirror and the face was smiling.
> "So this is how it is," he said to himself. (KL/EH 422.1/12, insert to 11–2nd insert to 11)

In his question, if not in the answer, he is strongly reminiscent of Jake Barnes, who, like David, was an aviator in the war. Jake has a similar mirror moment in *The Sun Also Rises*. In love with Brett Ashley (another rich and strange woman), but knowing he can never achieve sexual union with her because of his injury, he reads his mail and then looks at himself, naked, in the mirror:

> There were two letters and some papers . . . One was a bank statement. It showed a balance of $2432.60. I got out my check-book . . . The other letter was a wedding announcement. Mr. and Mrs. Aloysius Kirby announce the marriage of their daughter Katherine . . . It was a funny name . . . There was a crest on the announcement. Like Zizi the Greek duke. And that count. The count was funny. Brett had a title, too. Lady Ashley. To hell with Brett. To hell with you, Lady Ashley.
> . . . Undressing, I looked at myself in the mirror . . .
> . . . My head started to work. The old grievance. Well, it was a rotten way to be wounded and flying on a joke front like the Italian. In the Italian hospital we were going to form a society. . . . That was where the liaison colonel came to visit me. That was funny. That was about the first funny thing. I was all bandaged up. (30–31)

Psychoanalytic critics make much of this moment; it is an evocative one (despite the fact that Jake's injury was a common aviator injury in World War I; David references such injuries in *The Garden of Eden*, quoting the Lydia Pinkham song, "Vive le cast iron seal the pilots best friend for who would have his cock or balls shot free so that he could no proper part of England be" [KL/EH 422.1/29, 30, insert to 30]). These critics often overlook

Jake's mail, however—a society wedding invitation (as a maimed man he can never marry Brett Ashley) and his bank statement (as a checkbook-balancing working man he can never marry Lady Ashley). He then looks in the mirror and confirms what he knows. He can never make love to Brett. He may be fertile; he can experience desire, but he is not virile.

Having confirmed his maleness, his virility, David then proceeds to lecture himself for two pages, echoing "Up in Michigan" with the repeated phrase "You like it" (and directly refuting the assertion in "The Three-Day Blow" that "Once a man's married he's absolutely bitched" [90], which he had evidently begun to suspect):

> "You like it," he said and it was true. . . . ^"That's how you feel. You like it."^ He looked into the mirror and he thought about the girl in Biarritz and of Catherine as he had just left her asleep and it was true ^And ^he liked it. That's what was true.^^
>
> . . ."All right You like it," he said. "Now go through with the rest of it whatever it is and don't ever say anyone tempted you or that anyone bitched you ^Because /you like it/ it's like that girl in Biarritz and you like it."^
>
> He looked at the face that was ^now^ no longer strange to him at all ^but it was his face now^ and said "You hired out to do it ^all this^ and you like it. ^You hired out after it happened in Grau du Roi. Remember that. Keep that straight. After the first change. Not before.^ So go ahead and like it.
>
> . . . He . . . into town and brought the papers and came back as intact as when he left. (KL/EH 422.1/12, 12–13; /deletions/; ^insertions^)

The repetition of the phrase "You like it" (three of which Hemingway added while drafting this section) in a scene of sexual arousal echoes a passage from his earliest surviving story, "Up in Michigan." There, Hemingway illustrated the virginal Liz Coates's sexual desire for Jim Dilworth by repeating the phrase "She liked it" at the beginning of nearly every sentence for an entire paragraph: "Liz liked Jim very much. She liked it the way he walked over from the shop and often went to the kitchen door to watch for him to start down the road. She liked it about his mustache. She liked it about how white his teeth were when he smiled. She liked it very much that he didn't look like a blacksmith. She liked it how much D. J. Smith and Mrs. Smith liked Jim. One day she found that she liked it the way the hair was black on his arms and how white they were above the tanned line when he washed up in the washbasin outside the house. Liking that made her feel funny" (59). David, unlike Jake Barnes, returns intact, the virility question settled in his favor.

The Garden of Eden answers its virility question in this moment, but the related fertility question is still unanswered, not to mention the questions raised about the conjunction between Catherine turning into a boy and her menstrual cycle. Hemingway was so careful about making the timing identical that it is possible that Catherine so regularly turned into a boy on the eve of menstruation in order to deny biologically determined aspects of gender; it is also tempting to speculate that her illness was hormonally linked (or exacerbated). Regardless, Catherine has menstruated twice in the last two months, each time having a major argument with David that seems to be about one thing but is actually about having a baby. Each of these major arguments refers almost exactly to Hemingway's early marriage or fertility tales.

The first argument takes place in Madrid, the day after she has turned herself into a boy, and the first day she insists on being a boy in public. That morning, "when they woke . . . they were both happy and the day was clear and fine. For a moment he did not remember" (KL/EH 422.1/9, 19; a moment reminiscent of "Ten Indians," which ends, "In the morning . . . he was awake a long time before he remembered that his heart was broken" [257]). Later that day, after David has thought about the "new country" and "the bones of the others" and has medicated his remorse with absinthe, Catherine joins him at the café. In this scene, Hemingway explicitly quotes "Hills Like White Elephants," "Cat in the Rain," and "The Sea Change" (and, obliquely, "Cross-Country Snow").

When Hemingway invokes "Hills Like White Elephants" in *The Garden of Eden,* the invocation occurs in a scene concerning the public consequences of sexual activity and is usually cross gendered (David usually echoes Jig), and the direction of thought changes from a focus on the future (Jig's preferred mode) to wishing for the past (David's). In the "Hills Like White Elephants" version of this conversation, Jig states,

> "I said we could have everything."
> "We can have everything."
> "No, we can't."
> "We can have the whole world."
> "No, we can't."
> "We can go everywhere."
> "No, we can't. It isn't ours any more."
> "It's ours."

"No, it isn't. And once they take it away, you never get it back."

"But they haven't taken it away." (213)

Giving voice to his remorse at their gender games, David tells Catherine that: "We can always go back where we started." Catherine replies "Of course we can and we will. Don't feel anything is gone. Nothing's ever gone. We can't lose anything" (KL/EH 422.1/10, 7). David is wrong; they cannot go back to where they started. As Jig says in "Hills Like White Elephants," "every day [they] make it more impossible" (213). Jig and David are *both* wrong about whether or not the consequences of their sexual actions will result in loss. Jig's companion is telling the truth when he says that "they haven't taken it away"; in "Hills Like White Elephants," she does not lose the baby ("it"). Catherine may believe that she and David "can't lose anything," but they, unlike Jig and her companion, not only can lose; they have already lost something. And Catherine, at least, will lose "everything."

In both scenes, Hemingway invokes the taste of absinthe in situations dominated by sexual consequences. David muses, "It's a very strange thing . . . This drink [absinthe] tastes exactly like remorse. It has the true taste of it and yet it takes it away" (KL/EH 422.1/10, 8). His focus on the taste of remorse references Jig's comment that "Everything tastes of licorice. Especially all the things you've waited so long for, like absinthe" (213). David embraces his "friend" the absinthe, which allows him to avoid his complicated morning-after feelings; Jig, after one sip of the *Anis del Toro* (which reminds her of absinthe), "put[s] the glass down." David embraces a temporary escape; Jig cannot escape her pregnancy and wants to embrace it if her companion agrees. In neither case is "it" taken away—David's remorse will grow, and Jig's pregnancy will go to term. But both must "wait and see" (213).

While David is echoing "Hills Like White Elephants," Catherine begins to echo "Cat in the Rain." His statement that she looks "radiant" (a word usually reserved for brides and pregnant women) makes her reply:

"It's a terrible word. But I am. They have the worst words for the loveliest things. Like ecstacy [*sic*]."

"Ecstacy is a name for a cat."

"It's a good name for a cat. A cat must like it with the esses."

. . . [Catherine:] "And Ecstacy is the name of a cat."

. . ."And Ecstacy is the name of a cat . . . Of course I'm happy. Ecstacy is the name of a cat." (KL/EH 422.1/10, 5–11)

The non sequitur quality of this exchange may be blamed on the absinthe, which both of them are drinking. Catherine's seizure on the cat motif, as insistent as the wife's "I want a cat. I want a cat now. If I can't have long hair or any fun I can have a cat" in "Cat in the Rain" (131) suggests that the cat may have a symbolic meaning for her. Several pages later, one learns that she has just gotten her period and now knows that she is not pregnant. David's comment that "Ecstacy is a good name for a cat" is doubtless a reference to his wife; the previous night, he had awakened "and felt her head /pushing/ stroking against him like a /cat/ small smooth animal" (KL/EH 422.1/9, 16; /deletions/). Although she is never called Cat, an obvious nickname for Catherine, the conjunction of her name and Catherine Barkley's in *A Farewell to Arms* is not incidental. Catherine Barkley's fertility will kill her. Catherine Bourne's apparent sterility will contribute to her madness (this scene is the first in the novel to raise it as a question, as I will discuss momentarily). Given the obvious sexual pun on "pussy," if Ecstacy is what David calls her while expressing his remorse, what place has she, really, in his life, beyond that of a sex toy?

Cats in Hemingway seem always to function as a leitmotif for female reproduction and pregnancy, especially in "Cat in the Rain" and the drafts of "Cross-Country Snow" (see chapter 1). These early stories contain similar moments:

> In the doorway stood the maid. She held a big tortoise-shell cat pressed tight against her and swung down against her body. ("Cat in the Rain," 131)
>
> The [pregnant waitress] . . . came into the room and picked up a cat that had slipped through when she brought in the wine and went out. ("Cross-Country Snow," KL/EH 345, 6)

Compare the opening of *The Garden of Eden:* "He was a heavy fish and he [the waiter] held him high against his chest with the fish's head under his chin and his tail flopping against his thighs" (KL/EH 422.1/1, 8).

This is the fish for which David wished he had the jig, or spoons; the waiter carries the fish "swung down" against his body. Fish in Hemingway's works often mirror the condition of the male protagonist. Santiago, in *The Old Man and the Sea,* calls the fish "brother"—he and the fish will both be reduced to skeletons by the end of the book. In "Big Two-Hearted River," the fish under the bridge must exert all their energy merely to remain motionless in the current. In that story, Nick likewise deploys all his energy to avoid thinking. In this early scene in *The Garden of Eden,* David, like the fish, has been hooked and landed—by Catherine.

But David has also hooked and landed Catherine—and the fish, held in the same position as the cat in "Cat in the Rain" and (perhaps) the cat in "Cross-Country Snow." Considered in the context of these four moments (including the initially obscure "Ecstacy is the name of a cat"), full-body contact with animals by maids and waiters in Hemingway's works indicates the conjunction of fertility, virility, and public acknowledgment of commitment. To say that in Hemingway's mind, at least, the wife in "Cat in the Rain" probably does want a baby seems reasonable, thus establishing the story as not only a marriage tale but a fertility tale as well. Furthermore, although Catherine and David in *The Garden of Eden* achieve sexual "ecstacy," that is all—they will never have a baby. After making love, David (like most of Hemingway's characters) feels "happy" but "hollow" or "empty"; biologically, Catherine will remain unfilled, and their union un(ful)filled (although not, as she believes, because she does not have a baby). This will become evident, by contrast, in the language Marita will later use to describe how she feels after making love with David. Speaking about the baby she believes they have just made, she tells him, "I just feel as though a whole tree was planted in me" (KL/EH 422.1/34, 15). Sex with Marita is reproductive; sex with Catherine is not.[19]

Catherine laments her lack of identity (outside of being the sexual partner who brings David ecstasy and remorse); and her lack of identity leads her abruptly—and revealingly—into a discussion of his writing. Echoing the wife in "Cat in the Rain" (who wants things—her own silver, a dining room table, etc.), Catherine asks, "Why wouldn't I be happy?" She states first what they are together ("We're handsome, young, have money, we're ideally suited to each other"), then what David is ("You're talented, will be famous" [the word "famous" will figure centrally as their marriage breaks down]). Then, however, she takes a darker, self-negating turn, with a list of what she is *not:*

> "I'm a noted what? Not horsewoman, not tennis player, not painter, not writer. What? Clubwoman, patroness of the arts, salon bitch? Member of the Paris colony? Niece of my uncle?"
> "Bon vivant," he said.
> "You're nice," she said. "I'll stop."
> "Talk," he said. "You were going fine."
> "I could see you storing it away. Do I help you as a writer David? We haven't thought about your career."
> "Fuck my career."

"I hope we haven't," she said. "We ought to save something for when we're old."

"Keep it up. You're helping me good now."

"No," she said. "Ecstacy is the name of a cat." (KL/EH 422.1/10, 11–12)

Her remark about his "storing it away" recalls the woman's comment to Phil in "The Sea Change" ("You've used it well enough" [304], possibly referring to Phil's exploiting their relationship in his writing), but whereas in that story it is a barbed comment about the past, in Catherine's case it looks forward—having no identity of her own, at least as defined by her class and gender, she hopes to be David's muse—and, as the narrative later reveals, the protagonist of his story.

Their argument continues and escalates until David asks Catherine to "hold it down" (i.e., not publicize their argument). Catherine immediately genders this request, implying that males, when they disagree, say nothing (which is ever the case in Hemingway), whereas "girls" must publish their emotions:

"Why should I hold it down? You want a girl don't you? Don't you want everything that goes with it? Scenes, hysteria, false accusations, temperament isn't that I? I'm holding it down. I won't make you uncomfortable in front of the waiter. I won't make the waiter uncomfortable. I'll read my damned mail. Can we send up and get my mail?"

"I'll go up and get it."

"I don't want to read it."

"Let me get it."

"No please don't go"

"I'll only be a minute"

"No. I shouldn't be here by myself."

"That's right," he said.

"You see? That's why I said to send for it."

"They wouldn't give a *botones* the key to the room. That's why I said I'd go." (KL/EH 422.1/10, 14–5)

This is another one of Hemingway's seemingly irrational marital spats (similar to the one in "Cat in the Rain," which begins with "I'll get it [the cat]" and ends with "Why don't you shut up and get something to read?" and also to the unspecified argument that contributes the underlying tension to "Out of Season"; see chapter 1). Here, however, Hemingway indicates that this one has at least a partial origin in unpredictable, mercurial female hormones:

"I'm over it," Catherine said. "I'm not going to act that way. Why should I act that way to you? It was ludicrous and undignified. It was so silly. I won't even ask you to forgive me. Besides I have to go up to the room anyway—"

"Now?"

"Because I'm a god-damned woman. I thought if I'd be a girl and stay a girl I'd have a baby at least. Not even that."

. . . [Catherine:] "We'll read our mail and be good nice intelligent tourists who are disappointed because they came to Madrid at the wrong time of year." (KL/EH 422.1/10, 16)

Catherine's "I'm a god-damned woman" and the similarity between this argument and those in "Cat in the Rain" and "Out of Season" (situationally echoed by being in Madrid "at the wrong time of year") combine to support fertility readings of these two stories.[20]

"A little more than a month" later, just long enough for Catherine's period to have been slightly late, they have another similarly structured fight (KL/EH 422.1/11, 1). Trouble again begins with Catherine's boredom (cf. "Cat in the Rain"), continues through her lack of identity (cf. "Cat in the Rain"), almost immediately raises the question of fertility, and then suddenly veers into David's writing in a way that undermines the authenticity of Catherine's behavior—David and the reader learn that she is consciously performing as a character in the honeymoon narrative he is writing.

[Catherine:] "If we'd had the damned baby I wouldn't want to have it around. Anymore than my parents wanted me around. They were honest about it."

"That's one thing we don't have to worry about today."

"No. And if you think we're going to a dirty french [*sic*] doctor and have him poke things inside of me and take your juices that belong to me and make slides of them and try to mess up our lives—"

"I hadn't thought of it."

"You should have let me go on. I was just beginning to warm up."

"You're my devil."

"Yes I am. And as for that fucking patter of little feet. Probably running to the stables to ask the garage man for an ax to kill mummy."

"Wouldn't the garage man give her a spanner?"

"What is a spanner?"

"For what they're always using them for it must be either a wrench or a tire iron."

"Be careful how you spell tyre," she said. "Have you got a spanner in the book?"

"Not yet." (KL/EH 422.1/11, 12–13)

Catherine is becoming obsessed with seeing her sea changes reflected in David's writing and in the mirror she will soon procure for the bar in their La Napoule residence, where they, as the only guests, are once again "out of season."

She continues:

"What's the book about?"

"I don't know yet."

"If you don't know nobody else ever will. Don't you think you should find out? Do you want me to tell you the plots of some good new books?" (KL/EH 422.1/11, 14)

David, determined to avoid this conversational direction, responds calmly, but with a double entendre that Catherine cannot miss, "I sort of find out a little more about this one each day."

Writing and Authorship

Catherine takes the hint for several pages but returns, via thoughts of the French fertility doctor, whom she calls a "semen stealer," to the book, and for the first time begins to insist on its publication (one of the final stages of her madness will involve her acting as its publisher in going to Picasso to ask him to illustrate it, thus publicizing its subject matter, if not its words).

"He's [the doctor] my enemy. David how far are you really on the book?"

"Pretty far."

... [Catherine:] "Write for me too," she said. "No matter if it's when I've been bad. Put in how much I love you."

"I'm nearly up to now."

"It should certainly be instructive. Nobody's ever written it have they?"

"I hope not."

"I hope not too. Can you publish it or would it be bad to?"

"I've only tried to write it." (KL/EH 422.1/11, 27)

David's reply is especially revealing if one understands, as Hemingway did, the difference between writing and authorship. By talking about publishing the narrative, Catherine is pushing him into authorship. When he states that he has "only tried to write it," he does not appear to answer the question she has asked (whether or not such a sexually explicit work could be published). David's answer is a direct one, though, if one accepts that writing and authorship are different roles in the process of textual production and that the time is not yet right for David to think as an author.

David has been carefully managing his readiness and his energy to write throughout *The Garden of Eden,* telling Catherine early on that to write he needs "to be by myself in my head and I don't want to be" (KL/EH 422.1/1, 11), and then, after Madrid, saying that it is time to start writing. Catherine's question about publication is intrusive. She does not understand the differences between writing and publishing, between being a writer and an author, among art, money, and reputation. She should, however, because she has already asked a similar question.

David had tried to explain these differences to her, in reference to painting, in chapter 3. During a conversation with Nick Sheldon and his wife, Nick refers to a picture he painted of Barbara as a "family picture." Catherine, who will later ask David for a published version of the honeymoon narrative to be her birthday present (422.1/11, 28), thus hearkens back to Hemingway's gift to Pauline, in 1927, of the "Hills Like White Elephants" manuscript. Catherine, who apparently does not understand or respect the difference between art and commodity, asks to buy the portrait. Barbara refuses. Catherine, in assuming that all art is for sale, has presumed too much; she is asking them to make public something that is private and to commodify their intimacies. Nick and Barbara seem willing to let this pass, but David, understanding the multiple levels of her insult, explains to her that a painter paints, and a dealer sells paintings; then, to drive his point home, he asks her, "Now do you want them to ask you about your finances?" Resenting his condescension, she responds vehemently: "Just because you wrote this morning and feel so damned self-righteous. Why do writers have to always be so self-righteous about writing? What is so holy and sacred about writing anyway? . . . You and your clippings" (KL/EH 422.1/4, chap. 3, pp. 5–6). That she chooses religious diction is telling, all the more so in light of Marita's referring to David's writing (the time he spends writing it, when it goes well) as a *mystère* (which translates literally as "mystery"; in French, however, *mystère* specifically and inescapably connotes the divine mysteries of Catholicism; KL/EH 422.1/29, 50–51). To David, there is something sacred (or sacred-like) about writing, especially writing the Africa fiction to which Marita refers.

Marita's understanding of the difference between writing in its private context and writing as the profession of authorship provides the counterpoint to Catherine's unwitting (and self-serving) insistence on art as a business. Because Marita understands the *mystère*, David lets her read his fiction (he has not let Catherine read either the fiction or the honeymoon narrative; he later learns that she has kept the extra key to his suitcase and not only read the narrative but shared it with Marita). Because Marita has read both, she understands the points of contiguity between the honeymoon and the writing. And because Marita has read both, she will accompany David on a drive after he learns that Catherine has burned his stories—she knows what he has lost, and why he has had to get away from Catherine.

Marita is, in a way, the Thea Elvsted to Catherine's Hedda Gabler.[21] Catherine's possible desire for a child is thwarted by her own (or perhaps David's) body; once it is evident that she will not have a child, she fixes her attention on publishing David's honeymoon narrative, finally aborting his Africa stories (as discussed earlier) by burning them, as Hedda does Lövborg's manuscript (which Thea refers to as their "child"), saying, "Now I am burning your child, Thea!—Burning it, curly-locks! Your child and Eilert Lövborg's. I am burning—I am burning your child" (Ibsen 470). Catherine does not consciously think of the Africa stories as David and Marita's child (at least not in the text; the burning happens "offstage"). However, her motives and Hedda's are similar. Hedda decides to burn the manuscript when she learns that Lövborg considers Thea, and not herself, his inspiration; Catherine, seeking herself in David's writing, does not find herself there. Catherine's jealousy is aroused not by Marita sharing David's bed, but rather by Marita's having read his stories.

Catherine does not witness the scene in which David tells Marita that "There are more [stories] since you've been here than in all [my life] the time before. Good ones, I mean" (422.1/29, 24). As Marita reads the stories, one learns that David "had never done this before with anyone and it was against everything he believed in about writing but he did not think of that . . . He could not help sharing what he had never shared and what he had believed could not and should not be shared" (422.1/29, 24). Marita then asks him "Can we make love and not care if we make a baby?" (422.1/29, 25). Later she asks if he had ever let people in in writing. He replies:

"Nobody ever all the way. Until you."

"Why me?"

"Because you knew about it and loved it. It's a secret and if you tell about it then it's gone. It's a *mystère*. But you know about it."

"It's a true *mystère*," the girl said. "The way they had true *mystères* in religion."

"I didn't have to tell you about it," David said. "You knew about it when I met you."

"I only really learned with the stories," the girl said. "It was like being allowed to take part in the *mystère*. Please David I'm not meaning to talk trash."

"It isn't trash. But we must be very careful not to ever say it to other people." (422.1/29, 50–51)

The way writing feels is a secret, only to be shared and understood, never published, never told. Perhaps this is why, when pressed in interviews about how he wrote, Hemingway would usually get frustrated and change the subject.

The nineteenth-century Hedda is the more cruel for understanding the *mystère*, for understanding that she is destroying "Thea's soul" (Ibsen 469) and a "child"; the twentieth-century Catherine, however, pushes the money question. "Weren't the stories worth a lot? I feel terribly about that and I'm going to make it up to you. Truly I am. That's one of the reasons I was going to Paris" (KL/EH 422.1/32, 6). Later she repeats:

"I'm really going to make it up to you about the stories, David," she said. "You mustn't worry about that. It's bothered me terribly and I know my responsibility. Please have confidence in me, David. You know I don't take it lightly don't you?"

"Don't mention it," David said.

"I'll find out and do exactly what I should."

"Just what is it that you propose to do?"

"I'll have their value determined and I'll have twice that amount paid into your bank."

"That sounds very generous," David said. "But you always were generous."

"I want to be just, David, and it's possible that they were worth, financially, much much more than they would be appraised at." (KL/EH 422.1/32, 9–10)

Her insult does not end here, however, and David, knowing her, knows it. In order to find out how much the stories are worth (and glossing over the fact that they no longer exist), she will talk to publishers—not incidentally the most powerful people in publishing—thus publishing what she has done and making a spectacle of their marriage (advertising it the way Hemingway risked doing with "A Canary for One"; see chapter 2), destroying not only David's writing but the privacy he needs in order to write. David asks her,

> "Who appraises these things?"
> "There must be people who do. There are people who appraise everything."
> "What sort of people?"
> "I wouldn't know, David. But I can imagine such people as the editor of *The Atlantic Monthly, Harper's, Le* [*sic*] *Nouvelle Revue Française.*"
> "Not *Blackwood's?*" David asked.
> "If you like," Catherine said. "I'd thought of your own publishers too to be absolutely fair."
> "I'm going out for a while," David said. (KL/EH 422.1/32, 10)

That she will talk to *his* publishers, that everyone who knows him professionally will know his private story, is the final insult, the final degradation.

In the virility-fertility strand that is the honeymoon story in *The Garden of Eden,* David comes to terms with his pleasure in Catherine's gender switching (which requires a concomitant switching on his part; when she is the boy, he plays her girl). Catherine, obsessed with the story of her transformation, which she represents publicly by wearing trousers and sporting a boy's haircut, does not understand that what to her is an expression of her identity is, to David, playing a role. And although he comes to understand that Catherine's roles are not roles at all but her identity, Catherine never comes to understand the opposite about David and his writing—that although his writing is his vocation, his identity, authorship is his professional role—and thus that she has not only risked his writing but threatens his career as well. In her self-absorbed obsession and her illness, she does not understand him at all.

Personal and Authentic—Andy

One section that was cut from the published version of *The Garden of Eden* addresses directly the distinction Hemingway drew between his Personal and Authentic writing. Although David Bourne is primarily a Personal writer (his two novels concern his experiences in the war and his childhood in Africa), Andrew Murray is an Authentic writer. (Andy was cut entirely in the Jenks edition, the only published version of *The Garden of Eden*.) Andy figures early in the novel, when he is first mentioned by Nick and Barbara Sheldon in the Hendaye section (Andy and David helped Nick find a dealer in Paris); he appears in person in the Madrid section (and again in a frame that Hemingway seems to have written later and discarded, in which Andy tells the story of David and Catherine to an unnamed girl in a Paris café ["The story of a story" KL/EH 422.2]).

Spilka suggests that Nick and Barbara are representations of Ernest and Hadley Hemingway of the Paris years, and that David and Catherine represent Ernest and Pauline Hemingway a few years later. Andy, too, is a version of Hemingway (360); although Spilka dismisses him as "square," his importance in the novel is not merely that of a nonparticipant in the androgynous hair experiments. No; as his writing is described (by himself and others), he emerges specifically as an echo of the Hemingway who wrote *Death in the Afternoon,* the book Hemingway's critics had least understood.

Andy describes his book for Catherine in a conversation with David:

[Andy:] "It's just about where I lived and the country and the people. . . . It tells about that part of the country."

"There's always somebody that loves Spain and knows about it and can write it," David said. "There was Borrow, and a man named Ford and now there's Andy. After Andy there will be someone else."

"It would be better if the Spaniards did it," Andrew said. "But when they won't there's always something that should be written. If you take it very slowly and only write what [is true] you know it can be quite interesting. It's a very complicated country. It will take all my life to get to know it at all. And sometimes I have to go away from it to write it. Then I get homesick [for it]." (KL/EH 422.1/6, 8)

Andy's description of his book encapsulates the two final versions of the last chapter of *Death in the Afternoon*—the excised chapter 20 from the galley proofs and the chapter as published.

88   THE BONES OF THE OTHERS

Both versions begin by telling about "the country and the people." Galley 78 begins, "It is a strange country, Spain"; the published version begins "If I could have made this enough of a book it would have had everything in it. The Prado"—where Catherine spends most of her time in Madrid—"the bare white mud hills . . . It would have had the change when you leave the green country" (270). The galleys continue: "If you care, physically, for a new country it will change under your eyes as a young woman changes. . . . Reading this over I find I lied in that I cared very much for the country around the Camargue"—le Grau du Roi, les Saintes-Maries-de-la-Mer, and Aigues-Mortes, where *The Garden of Eden* opens—"although how much of this can be laid to having gone there newly married I cannot say."

In the galleys, Hemingway next considers what it means to be an American who writes about Spain: "As an American I know it is very presumptuous of me to write about Spain and I have avoided diagnosing her soul. . . . Things do not belong to you that neither you nor your fathers have paid for." He continues, "it takes something more, something that has to be paid for a long time, something that talent, industry, astuteness cannot replace, to write the writing of a country that will last" (galley 79). In Andy's words, "It would be better if the Spaniards did it"; in Hemingway's, after Hemingway, there will be others.

In the published version, Hemingway ends by describing his process in writing *Death in the Afternoon,* which is similar to Andy's "If you take it very slowly and only write what [is true] you know it can be quite interesting": "The great thing is to last and get your work done . . . and write when there is something that you know; and not before; and not too damned much after. . . . if you can get to see it clear and as a whole. Then any part you make will represent the whole if it's made truly" (278).

Hemingway ends the galley version with what Andy mentions—the constant homesickness of the expatriate: "I returned to America, then, after living away from America . . . because I was physically lonesome for it . . . At the end of a year I went back to Europe for economic reasons . . . I had been very happy in America but I was always lonesome for Spain . . . Back in Spain and able to settle there I found that I did not want to live there but in America" (galley 80). Hemingway represents in Andy a version of himself that is a true foil for David; he writes nonfiction, he is poor, and because he writes nonfiction he is likely to stay poor (422.1/6, chap. 11, p. 1). But he loves his subject, and writing about it.

Others, however, do not find Andy's writing as valuable as David's. Catherine is the first to criticize it on the grounds of didacticism (a quality she also finds in Andy himself). The fact that she has not read it does not bother

her (a characteristic she shares with many of *Death in the Afternoon*'s detractors, as Hemingway anticipated [see chapter 4]). She tells Andy that one can't learn to like things (specifically, "oysters or Stravinsky or Klee"—or, by extension to *Death in the Afternoon,* bullfighting) "from a book." Then she dismisses his reply that "You have to have more than one book" with "I don't want to put you out of business, Andy" (KL/EH 422.1/6, 13–14). Catherine makes the assumption Hemingway's critics had been making since *The Sun Also Rises,* the same assumption David's critics make in the reviews his editors send him: that book and man are interchangeable, that the public representation of identity is an accurate reflection of identity.

Andy has three sensitive points, all of which respond to the critical and financial failure of *Death in the Afternoon* (and the bitterness that Hemingway began to feel toward Pauline after its publication). The first is that his book is nonfiction, the second is money, and the third is that everyone expects him, because he is a writer, to be a novelist. When David tells him that "The money is [Catherine's]," Andy's reserved façade cracks. "Don't talk to me about your finances. I'm not a damned novelist" (422.1/6, 2). Catherine, meanwhile, has wondered whether Andy or David is the better writer; the narration is quick to assure the reader that "Actually at the time one was about as good as the other" (KL/EH 422.1/6, 1). Hemingway's professional anxiety emerges here; it is the anxiety borne of public pressure throughout the 1930s to write novels. (To this extent, in his dismissal of Andy and the writing strand of *The Garden of Eden,* Spilka misses half the point.)

Two of David's conversations reveal that Andy's writing, understood in Hemingway's lexicon, is merely Authentic; thus its value will not be appreciated. David himself tells Andy that "You're . . . a meticulous observer. Nobody can say you are not a serious writer. You gleam with seriousness. It glows on every page" (KL/EH 422.1/6, 9). The phrase "meticulous observer" identifies Andy's writing, and much of *Death in the Afternoon,* as Authentic, the term that Hemingway used to refer to things he had witnessed, observed, overheard, or seen. The value placed on such writing by general readers (or bad critics) is voiced by the Colonel, with whom David discusses Andy and his work:

> [David:] "Do you get along with Andy?"
> [Colonel:] "Why shouldn't I? He can't write but neither can I. Only I happen to know it."
> "He can write."
> "Don't be stupid. It takes something more than diligence and dedication and *métier*." (KL/EH 422.1/6, 25)

David's decision not to publish the honeymoon narrative is implicit in this discussion of Andy's writing, and he knows it from the start. Although he later answers Catherine's pressure to publish it with "It's not a novel . . . It's an account" (KL/EH 422.1/11, 29), his first thought after he begins to write it, with the "five finger exercise" about the Sheldons in Paris, is to question whether it has any meaning for him. "But do you really give a damn about it? No. Let someone else write it. Andy knows it better than you do . . . You were taking it from him today. You cheap crook. It's his story. Let Andy write it" (KL/EH 422.1/5, 6). Hemingway considered doing just that when he wrote the Andy framing device, marked on the manuscript as "The story of a story." But that was one layer too many even for Hemingway; that section of *The Garden of Eden* remains unfinished.

Just as Andy and David comprise the two sides of Hemingway's writing, Nick Sheldon produces the same two kinds of paintings: Personal and Authentic. In painting, though, the values are reversed. His portrait of Barbara is personal; he paints her as he experiences her, as he feels love for her, as she "means" to him. The works he sends to his dealer, however, are authentic—he tries to capture things that no painter has captured before, things he sees, things that present a technical challenge to him: capturing the light in the water at the change of the tide.

Hemingway had long said that he tried to write as Cézanne painted landscapes; the critical confusion he caused by doing so haunted him for his entire career. The generic status of his work (Is it autobiography? journalism? fiction?) and his resistance to the demands of his public (for novels, always novels) were central questions in his professional life. In *The Garden of Eden,* he addressed the moment when these questions began to affect his writing and his reputation by referring explicitly to those texts whose thematics he ultimately identified as centering around publication: the early fertility and virility tales, and *Death in the Afternoon,* in which he proffered his metacritical take on publication—the dangers art production posed to art and artist.

CHAPTER FOUR

A PILGRIM'S PROGRESS INTO HELL

Death in the Afternoon and the
Problem of Authorship

All art is only done by the individual.
  —*Death in the Afternoon*

It is always a mistake to know an author.
  —*Death in the Afternoon*

The critic, out on a limb, is more fun to see than a mountain lion.
  —Ernest Hemingway

In *Death in the Afternoon,* Ernest Hemingway locates public, or published, art within a discursive matrix that is at once individual, artistic, aesthetic, professional, social, and cultural. He insists that "All art is only done by the individual" (99) but admits the matrix of publication as a necessity without which art (whether bullfighting or writing) cannot reach its public. On nearly every page he describes and critiques this matrix for the uncomfortable compromises it works on bullfighting and on its participants. In *Death in the Afternoon,* Hemingway metacritically argues that bullfighting—and, by analogy, any published art form—comprises a symbiotic dialogue between an artist and the public. This dialogue consists of the exchange of fiscal, cultural, and critical capital; the nature of the exchange, Hemingway insists, inevitably introduces mutations to the art form and to the artist. Against such mutations he proposes knowledge: specifically, a knowledgeable public.

Death in the Afternoon's Author–Old Lady dialogues are central to Hemingway's metacritical and pedagogical agendas. In these dialogues, Hemingway deconstructs the discursive exchange between an artist and art's public to illustrate the dangers intrinsic to that exchange. He first illustrates how his narrator, a writer, becomes, additionally, a character named Author through interaction with a lowest-common-denominator public (personified by another character, the Old Lady). He then instructs his readers to judge the Author's product as lacking in quality when compared to that of the narrator. Within Hemingway's logic, writer and author are necessarily connected but not synonymous: the writer is the individual artist—someone who *does*—whereas authorship is but a professional role, distinguishable from the writer by being no less a product of writing than the characters a writer creates.[1] When Hemingway began writing *Death in the Afternoon,* he was already aware of the extent to which he was becoming a brand-name author (a celebrity he would both court and resist for the rest of his career), and he had begun to glimpse how potentially detrimental the interest created by his public persona might be to his private writerly self, to his writing, and to his readers' experience of that writing.

Death in the Afternoon's Author–Old Lady dialogues were designed in part to alleviate a problem that the book as a whole was destined to exacerbate: the inescapable and multivalent problem of being "Ernest Hemingway, author." Hemingway's growing disdain for the mechanisms of art production, and consequently for his own implication in them, manifests in the text in three related ways: first, in his analogies between bullfighting and writing, or, more precisely, in the conflicts between art and business that both bullfighting and writing share; second, in his distinctions between the quality of artistic endeavor and the decay to which it is inevitably susceptible within the processes of art publication; and, finally, in his somewhat idealistic faith in education (of audience, by artist) as the means by which to check the decadent trends in art perpetuated by the economic mechanisms of art production, in bullfighting, in writing, and by implication, in all published or public art forms.

Hemingway understood the problem of authorship (or, as he first called it, "professional writing") from two angles. By the time he began writing *Death in the Afternoon,* the success of his first two novels, and his quasi-autobiographical tone had begun to shift the focus of Hemingway criticism from product to person. The second angle, which complicates the first, is the linguistic convention that obfuscates the distinction between product and person—using a writer's name either to reference the person or to metonymously signify the writing.[2] A further complication, the one around which the metacriticism implicit in the Author–Old Lady dialogues coalesces, lies in common and sometimes critical usage of the word "author," a word that may refer to the private man, the creative writer, and/or to the intrinsically public roles the man/writer plays in relation to his work. Thus criticism of Hemingway (his writing) may morph into criticism of Hemingway (the person) without any linguistic cues to alert the reader—and sometimes the critic—that the critical terrain has shifted. And although the terms "Hemingway" and "criticism" remain the same, the connotations and the stakes change dramatically as the shift occurs, especially for Ernest Hemingway. His role as a professional writer (someone who is implicated within and dependent on the mechanisms of art production and its related receptive discourses) forms the subtext of the Author–Old Lady dialogues, perhaps the least understood formal element of *Death in the Afternoon.*

The ambiguity of the term "author" (and, by implication, "Hemingway") accounts for much of the difficulty of *Death in the Afternoon.* Hemingway used the book as an opportunity to address this ambiguity and to underscore the dangers he locates therein. He provides two important signposts to indicate that these dangers are his object of inquiry. First, he creates an abstract character called Author, and secondly, he changes genres when that character appears. By using the labeling conventions of drama (in which a character's name precedes each line) to differentiate the Author–Old Lady dialogues from the rest of the text, Hemingway underscores that this Author is as much an artificially constructed character as the Old Lady. Much of what is odd in *Death in the Afternoon* begins to come clear once one realizes that authorship and publication are as central to the book as bullfighting is, and as applicable to bullfighting as to writing.

Hemingway's metacritical project resides in his subtle analogy between the art and business of bullfighting and the art and business of writing. Hemingway's generic term for bullfighters and writers is "artists"; his generic term for what they do is "art." Bullfighters and writers are artists, honing and developing their art; matador and author are professional titles referring to the roles these artists play in the negotiations that bring that art to a public. Hemingway's is a modernist allegory; he achieves it formally (by juxtaposition) and generically (by switching from expository prose to dramatic dialogue to short fiction), without warning or overt explanation.

The explanation resides in the formal presentation of these dialogues as a play. The Author character in these dialogues is initially indistinguishable from the narrator and has thus historically been mistaken for the author of the book. As the dialogues develop, though, Hemingway separates the Author from the narrator, thus revealing the Author as a character. The Author is not so much unmasked as revealed to be a mask worn by Hemingway, the mask superimposed on his writerly identity by public—especially critical—

perception. By naming this masking character Author, Hemingway aims for several ends: (1) to distinguish between writer and author (a difficult task); (2) to remind his reviewers that their business was to address his writing, not his image (a consummation devoutly to be wished); (3) to reveal his reviewers' inadequacies where warranted (a plan that backfired); and (4) to argue that what should matter most—to himself, to his reviewers, and to his readers—is the quality of his writing, not his public persona.

The apostrophic nature of these characters (their burlesque personifications of single character traits) further refines Hemingway's generic distinctions and clarifies his project. The dialogues are not merely a dramatic script; further analysis indicates that Hemingway presents them as a morality play that unfolds over nine episodes—a deliberate structural allusion to Dante's *Inferno*, in which the blind Virgil guides the pilgrim on a tour of hell. Once these generic and structural allusions are perceived, Hemingway's liberal deployment of intricate allusions throughout the text places his metacritical project in bold relief. *Death in the Afternoon*'s Author–Old Lady dialogues comprise a morality play, Hemingway's Sermon on the Mount against those scribes and Pharisees intrinsic to and implicated within discourses of art production.

Because *Death in the Afternoon*'s metacritical morality play comprises Hemingway's response to specific extratextual circumstances, however, an explication of the embedded play's structure and internal logic best begins, likewise, outside the text with a reconstruction of the conditions that first crystallized Hemingway's understanding of the problem of authorship and then catalyzed his response.

Hemingway first identified the negative effects of authorship after having endured the process of publishing *A Farewell to Arms*, although he had begun to suspect them years earlier. In a letter to his editor, Max Perkins, Hemingway complained about the changes he had been asked to make in order to see that novel into print. Although these concessions were relatively minor (replacing profanity with blank lines and hedging on certain anatomical references), Hemingway objected on principle, concluding: "I have become a Professional Writer . . . Than which there isn't anything lower" (quoted in Bruccoli and Trogdon 119).

Necessary concessions, however galling, did not provide Hemingway's only impetus toward a pedagogical crusade for artist-audience solidarity against the decadent effects of art production on art and artist. By the late 1920s, he had begun to receive invitations to write celebrity articles for magazines (invitations he would soon begin to accept). One such invitation came from Henry Goddard Leach, the editor of the *Forum* magazine. Leach wrote

Hemingway two letters that bracketed the 1929 publication of *A Farewell to Arms.* The first addressed him as a creative writer, the second as a public figure, as an author. Leach's letters so irritated Hemingway that in response he wrote or modified three short texts, all related to *Death in the Afternoon.* The first letter resulted in the short story "The Sea Change" and in two un-published pieces—one on bullfighting (KL/EH 681A) and one on a soldier's death in the First World War (KL/EH 734–5), topically related to "A Natural History of the Dead" (Smith, *Guide* 223). Both the timing and the wording of Leach's second letter suggest that it may have inspired the creation of the Author–Old Lady dialogues; at the very least, it contributed directly to the Author's introduction to "A Natural History of the Dead," the short story he tells the Old Lady in chapter 12.[3]

In his first letter, dated June 28, 1929 (and thus prior to the publication of *A Farewell to Arms*), Leach requested a short story "of about two-thousand words in length" and gave instructions as to its form: "As the FORUM reaches not only trained readers but the general public the story must contain narrative or at least plot. In other words it must not be merely a sketch."[4] Paul Smith notes that "in some forty words the editor managed to raise Hemingway's ire with misconceptions of the reading public, narrative or plot, and what is 'merely' a sketch" (*Guide* 223). Worse, he presumed to tell Hemingway how to write.

Hemingway predictably turned combative. His first response to Leach in-troduces an (unpublished) series entitled "Unsuited to Our Needs," stating, as Smith notes, "'Let us see what we can do in twelve hundred and sixty-two words'—the word count on his fair copy of 'The Sea Change'" (*Guide* 223; KL/EH 680 and 681). In this story, a woman is leaving her male lover for a woman; the narrative obliquely suggests that her reasons and the man's reac-tion may have something to do with writing and publication. The word count links "The Sea Change" to Leach's letter, thus supporting Robert Fleming's argument that the male lover, Phil, whose profession is never mentioned, is a writer who holds nothing sacred but is compelled to publish intimacies that for most people remain private. Fleming's argument is based on the woman's line, "We're made up of all sorts of things. You've known that. You've used it well enough" ("Sea Change" 304; Fleming, "Perversion" 216). How Phil has "used" this knowledge is less important to understanding "The Sea Change" than to understanding how the compulsion to write and to publish was be-ginning to erode Hemingway's personal privacy in the early 1930s.

Hemingway used everything in his writing, deploying his experience and his perceptions of others as fodder for his pen (especially in those stories he called Personal). Because his writing was good enough to earn him a wide readership, he had created an interest in himself that would eventually impede the freedom he needed to garner that experience.[5] Worse, critics were starting to judge him rather than his writing, thus potentially alienating him from the readership he desired—those who would value his writing over his celebrity. These were subtle distinctions that were as important to him as their blurring was inevitable for nearly everyone else. Although at this stage in his career what would now be termed media attention was more of an irritant than the spectacle it would later become, one thing is certain: he bridled at attempts to censor or shape his material and style. Hemingway did not need—and clearly did not like—to be told how to write. How he wrote was still a private matter, and if "The Sea Change" is any indication, a touchy one. It was not (yet, to him) an object for direct public consumption.

Leach's second letter, dated May 2, 1930, was written after the publication of *A Farewell to Arms* and its reviews; by then, Hemingway had started to write *Death in the Afternoon.*[6] This letter touched an even more sensitive nerve. In it, Leach does not presume to tell the author of *A Farewell to Arms* how to write; instead—and to Hemingway, more intrusively—he tells him what to write:

> I am writing to place before you a suggestion which I hope and believe will be worthy of your serious consideration.
>
> As editor of The FORUM magazine, I have been publishing each month . . . an article by some well known scientist, philosopher, or author in which each of these people has attempted to set forth his intimate beliefs . . . Among those who have contributed . . . are . . . Theodore Dreiser, Irving Babbitt, John Dewey, Sir Arthur Keith, James Trunslow Adams, H. L. Mencken, and Dr. Albert Einstein. You will see by this list that most of these contributors are elderly men.
>
> . . . To put it briefly, what we want from you is a statement of your personal credo, your convictions and beliefs concerning the nature of the world and of man. It would necessarily be suggestive since it would have to touch intimately on your own hopes and fears, the mainspring of your faith or the promptings of your despair.
>
> For such an article . . . The FORUM offers you $500.

Even had Hemingway ignored the closing insult (that he would be willing to bare his soul for $500), this letter was grating. Hemingway disliked Mencken, who, as coeditor of *American Mercury,* had rejected several of his early stories (Reynolds, *Paris* 234–35). Leach's use of titles and honorifics was pretentious, his pointing out the uniform age of the eminent personages condescending.

And with its name-dropping, Leach's letter pandered to Hemingway's new status as a public figure—a successful author—to the detriment of his status as a writer. Why should Ernest Hemingway's intimate feelings matter more to readers than his fiction writing?

Leach's requests and instructions provide the sounding board from which *Death in the Afternoon*'s Author–Old Lady dialogues echo. His request for a "personal credo" to address "the nature of the world and of man" and to reveal "the mainspring of [his] faith or the promptings of [his] despair" is reflected in the Author's anticipation of the Old Lady's criticism (specifically, in chap. 12, p. 132) and by his anticipation of her desire for a different kind of story with different content:

> [Author:] What would you like to have? More major truths about the passions of the race? . . . A few bright thoughts on death and dissolution? Or would you care to hear about the author's experience with a porcupine during his earliest years . . . ?
>
> [Old Lady:] Please, sir, no more about animals to-day.
>
> [Author:] What do you say to one of those homilies on life and death that delight an author so to write?
>
> [Old Lady:] I cannot truly say I want that either. (132–33)

In this exchange, Hemingway turns the tables on Leach and on others of similar ilk who would preempt his creative agency: the Author does just that to the Old Lady's agency, granting her only enough room to protest his suggestions weakly before he steamrolls her with even more outrageous ones, culminating in his giving her "A Natural History of the Dead"—a story she is guaranteed not to like, despite the fact that it meets her criteria of having "conversation" and being something "of a sort I've never read, amusing, yet instructive" (133). Although her criteria differ from those of Leach's general readers, she, like Leach, gives writing instructions: Leach's demand for "narrative, or at least plot," has become her request for "conversation," or at least novelty.

Despite the fact that the Old Lady interrupts the narrative of "A Natural History of the Dead" by complaining that it is "not amusing" (137) and by wondering, halfway through it, when it will start (140) (an effective riposte to Leach's directive about "narrative, or at least plot"), she persists in asking for something she will like. Her request recalls Leach's second letter in that she, too, tells the Author what to write, and she, too, asks not for fiction but memoir. Having learned her lesson about the Author's fiction with "A Natural History of the Dead," she asks instead for stories that the Author knows about the "unfortunate people" (by which she means homosexuals) in the Paris cafés. Like Leach (in his second letter), she wants titillation, not art.

The Author complies and delivers an anecdote, but only after he has warned her that it will "lack drama as do all tales of abnormality since no one can predict what will happen in the abnormal while all tales of the normal end much the same" (180). Undaunted, she insists, and quite predictably, she dislikes this story, finding the content boring and the craft weak because it lacks the obvious "wow" with which stories ended "in her youth" (182). She cannot be satisfied: she asks for a story and is disappointed that it is not an anecdote; she insists on an anecdote and, having been warned that it is not a story, is still disappointed that it is not a story. Her final judgment is that the Author is no good, and his final judgment on her is to have her thrown out of the book (190).

When she exits, the Author character also disappears—revealing that his existence depended on hers. The voice that delivers news of this ejection may seem to be the Author's, but since the first-person plural is employed, the narrative identity is changing. "Where is the Old Lady? She's gone. *We* threw her out of the book, finally. A little late you say? Yes, perhaps a little late. . . . Shall we try to raise the general tone?" (190; emphasis added). This "we" may merely continue the pompous tone of the Author, yet both Author and narrator were, previously, "I." The plural refers to the momentary hybridity of the narrative voices—Author and writer. After this brief passage, the plural disappears and, with it, halfway through the book, the reader has seen the last of the Author.

With the abrupt disappearance of the Author–Old Lady dialogues, the motivation behind their inclusion becomes clear. Hemingway constructed them as a response to editors like Henry Goddard Leach and critics (by which Hemingway meant reviewers) like Aldous Huxley. Immediately following the announcement of the Old Lady's departure, the narrator specifically addresses a critical passage from Huxley and counterattacks on the grounds of pretension, dismissiveness, and formulaic definitions of what constitutes good writing: the performance of one's education and cultural capital.

Understanding Hemingway's extratextual motivation is but half the challenge. The specifics of how Hemingway prepares the reader for chapter 17's showdown with Huxley warrant close attention, as these specifics constitute Hemingway's simultaneous delivery, deconstruction, and judgment of the performativity required of authors by the "blind guides" like Leach and Huxley, the "children of them which killed the prophets" (Matthew 23:31).

Hemingway opens the book with lessons for the novice spectator regarding the mutating compromises that an uneducated public can unwittingly force on an art form. In chapter 1, he illustrates the dangers of audience ignorance in terms of the horses in the bullring, whose disemboweling was then the object of public concern. He reports that "These visceral accidents, as I write this, are no longer a part of the Spanish bullfight, as under the government of Primo de Rivera it was decided to protect the abdomens of the horses with a sort of quilted mattress designed in the terms of the decree 'to avoid those horrible sights which so disgust foreigners and tourists'" (7). But, he notes, although the sights are avoided, the mattresses "in no way decrease the pain suffered by the horses; they take away much of the bravery from the bull, . . . and they are the first step toward the suppression of the bullfight. The bullfight is a Spanish institution; it has not existed because of the foreigners and tourists, but always in spite of them and any step to modify it to secure their approval, which it will never have, is a step towards its complete suppression" (8).

Hemingway is clearly subscribing to the well-wrought urn definition of art (that no single element constitutes the whole, but all affect it): "If [the audience senses] the meaning and end of the whole thing even when they know nothing about it; feel that this thing they do not understand is going on, the business of the horses is nothing more than an incident. If they get no feeling of the whole tragedy naturally they will react emotionally to the most picturesque incident . . . The aficionado . . . may be said, broadly, then, to be one who has this sense of the tragedy and ritual of the fight so that the minor aspects are not important except as they relate to the whole" (8–9). The lesson for the novice spectator is clear. It is not "You must love bullfighting," but, rather, "If you cannot judge the whole, do not base your judgment of the whole on parts whose connections you do not see." And, more urgently, "Do not demand the removal or modification of those parts you do not understand or that, for reasons unrelated to the whole, you disapprove of." In the economy of art, such partial judgments can lead to changes on the whole that will detract from the experience of those who understand and appreciate the work of art in its entirety.

Hemingway's concerns over the damages wrought by a financially powerful but artistically uninformed audience applied equally to bullfighting and to his own art, given his experience publishing *A Farewell to Arms,* which prompted his "professional writer" complaint to Perkins. Scribner's had objected to his use of the word "fucking" in that text on legal and moral grounds, but Hemingway was quick to perceive the financial reality that at best coexisted with these grounds and at worst constituted the truth behind them. The analogy between literary censorship (so as not to alienate squeamish book buyers) and the padding of the horses (to placate squeamish foreigners) is clear: both changes pandered to an audience whose power lay in its pocketbook.

By 1930, Hemingway imagined himself fairly free of such pressure. On the basis of his previous successes (*The Sun Also Rises* and *A Farewell to Arms*), and with the financial backing of his wealthy uncle-in-law Gus Pfeiffer, he felt that he could finally write the book he had planned for years, without worrying about critical or popular success. For the first time in his career, he believed that he could enact his own authority with little concern for the consequences. He relied on his brand-name status to bring an unlikely book on an unlikelier topic into public circulation, presuming that at least some of his audience would perceive the complex analogical project beneath *Death in the Afternoon*'s deceptive simplicity. This technique had won him critical acclaim for his short fiction; this plan would, however, backfire.

Hemingway introduces the subject of writing and authorship on the first page of *Death in the Afternoon*. He announces that he will try "only to tell honestly the things I have found true . . . [to] be altogether frank, or to try to be." He expects that his critics and his readers will judge him, rather than his work: "if those who read this decide with disgust that it is written by some one [*sic*] who lacks their, the readers', fineness of feeling I can only plead that this may be true" (1). Anticipating this personal judgment, which is irrelevant, he presents the only criterion that he considers valid: a reader "can only truly make such a judgment when he, or she, has seen the things that are spoken of and knows truly what their reactions to them would be" (1). At the outset, Hemingway acknowledges the widening gap between his writerly goals and his professional image, a gap created by the fact that his critics were paying too much attention to his public persona and not enough to his writing.

Hemingway was setting a trap. "If you pay the right kind of attention as you read this book," he implies, "you will understand my writing. But if you bring to it only preconceptions (as people are wont to do with bullfighting, and as critics are wont to do with my work), not only will you miss the point, but you will miss a point I have made so obvious that you will be proved the fool."

Because this presumably nonfiction text begins in first-person singular narration, readers may assume that the narrator's voice and Ernest Hemingway's are one and the same. Soon, however, Hemingway begins to draw a subtle, practical distinction between the author and the narrative "I":

This that has been written . . . is not put in because of a desire of the author to write about himself and his own reactions, considering them as important and taking delight in them because they are his, but rather to establish the fact that the reactions were instant and unexpected. (8)

and

I did not become indifferent to the fate of the horses through . . . callousness. (8)

In these adjacent sentences, "the author" and "I" both seem to refer to Hemingway. But the awkwardness of the passive construction in the first sentence ("this that has been written . . . is not put in") contrasts so sharply with the active directness of the second ("I did not become indifferent") that the two sentences command the reader's close attention. The first anticipates criticism that the passive author will receive (that is, that he has an ego problem); the second asserts agency. Hemingway will clarify this distinction (the author as a passive, receptive role as opposed to "I" as an active force) as the book progresses, according to the following system: "I" experience, "the writer" writes, and "the author" is a public, professional role, a two-dimensional mask that may be mistaken for the writer and the man.

Before the narrative voice splits into the two distinct voices of the writer and the Author, it describes with careful precision the process whereby experience becomes writing. The narrator states that "the problem was one of depiction" (the writer's task), and to illustrate the point, he recounts what it was that was important about Domingo Hernandorena's goring: "waking in the night I tried to remember what it was that seemed just out of my remembering and that was the thing that I had really seen and, finally, remembering all around it, I got it. When he stood up, his face white and dirty and the silk of his breeches opened from waist to knee, it was the dirtiness of the rented breeches, the dirtiness of his slit underwear and the clean, clean, unbearably clean whiteness of the thigh bone that I had seen" (20). This is clearly a writer's voice, finding and focusing on the detail that enables him to transform experience into writing. This voice will change with the appearance of the Old Lady in chapter 7, and it will eventually give way to a caricature named Author, from whom one learns little about writing, the writer, or bullfighting (or, finally, anything but his scorn for the Old Lady).

The inclusion of the Old Lady—her ignorance, her preconceptions, and her judgments—enables Hemingway to represent the medium of exchange between artist and public, an interactive but usually inarticulate medium that necessarily changes the artist, and not for the better. Like the introduction of the padding on the horses, these interactions represent a mutation of form. Textually, they occur within a mutation of form (a Bunyanesque interplay of prose and drama); they inherently present a mutation of form (in which the narrator becomes the Author); and they address a mutation of form (in the Old Lady's criticism of "The Natural History of the Dead" and the anecdote about homosexuals in Paris).

Initially, the Author–Old Lady dialogues illustrate the transitional moment at which a writer (the narrator) assumes an additional role, the discursive nexus represented by the character of the Author. Subsequently, with their structural and thematic allusions to Dante's *Inferno* (as well as to the Bible, John Bunyan's *Pilgrim's Progress,* and Shakespearean tragedy), they deliver Hemingway's consequent judgment on the relative value of these two roles within the process of art production.

In the nine Author–Old Lady dialogues, several things happen:

1. The narrative voice gradually splits into two, one retaining its original tone and purpose (the discussion of bullfighting), and the other becoming, by chapter 9, an abstract character named Author.
2. This character introduces the Old Lady to several aspects of professional bullfighting, professional writing, and their attendant dangers.
3. The Old Lady character becomes a literary critic, then a personal one, and confuses the two. Meanwhile the Author character becomes abrasive, smug, and condescending.
4. The Author and the Old Lady are thrown out of the book by the original narrator.

The first-person narration of the first six chapters slides invisibly into the lines of the Author (63). Later, however, Hemingway sets the Author's lines apart from the rest of the text as he does with the Old Lady's throughout (the Author is first labeled on page 93). The deliberate invisibility of this transition emphasizes Hemingway's point—that the narrator/writer has invisibly (and inevitably) become, additionally but distinctly, the Author through his interaction with his public, represented by the Old Lady. He further underscores this transition, topically, in the Author's second labeled line, which addresses a similar professional transition: "[the restaurant] is full of politicians who are becoming statesmen as one watches them" (93). "Politician" is their métier; the "statesmen" label is their professional role, here endowed by the gaze of their public (the watching audience). Only in retrospect is it obvious that the narrator/writer has similarly become the Author as—and because—the Old Lady watches him. The Old Lady remains static throughout the dialogue; the narrator-cum-writer devolves. In becoming the Author through his engagement with her as his public, he literally performs the book's central premise that economic pressures and publication endanger art and the artist, making them both susceptible to decadence (in the sense of decay). The identification of the problem of authorship and its adherent dangers is exacerbated by the fact that words, like "decadence" and "authorship," have "from loose using . . . lost their edge" (71).

The dialogues' characters first appear in chapter 7. At the end of chapter 6, Gabriel's trumpet sounds, denotatively heralding the start of the bullfight, but allegorically heralding judgment day: "The president gives a signal with his handkerchief, the trumpet sounds and the very serious, white-haired, white old man, his name is Gabriel . . . unlocks the door of the toril and pulling heavily on it runs backward to expose the low passageway that shows as the door swings open" (61–62). Through this narrative door, the Author and Old Lady enter, she heedless of Gabriel's trumpet and of the sign that appears over the textual doorway (although nowhere in the text): "Abandon all hope, ye who enter here" (Dante, *Inferno* 3.7).

Nine Author–Old Lady dialogues record the Old Lady's pilgrimage into the world of bullfighting; they also record the narrator's descent into the hell of authorship. Chapters 1–6, which precede the dialogues, belong to the uncommitted, those who, never having seen a bullfight, remain in limbo. Chapter 7 begins, "At this point it is necessary that you see a bullfight" (63). The Old Lady enters.

Her "guide," "Master," and "Author" (as Dante's pilgrim addresses Virgil [1.85]) introduces her to several things about professional bullfighting, professional writing, and their attendant vices, or sins. Although these vices do not map sequentially onto all Dante's circles of hell, most of them come close. The allusive structure of the Author–Old Lady dialogues combines with a religious lexicon (sin, messiah, etc.), apostrophic characters, and scattered references to theatre (to *Hamlet, Romeo and Juliet*, "the three acts in the tragedy of the bullfight" [98], etc.) to identify these sections as a morality play: a didactic genre involving "the dramatic presentation of a sermon" (*Benét's* 664), in this case Hemingway's Sermon on the Mount against critics who "jest at scars" yet "who never felt a wound" (i.e., live as parasites off the work of artists without ever attempting to create art themselves [103; Shakespeare, *Romeo* 2.2.1]). Each dialogue concerns a separate sin, vice, or danger to which the publishing process subjects the artist, whether bullfighter or writer:

Table 2. The Circles of Hell

Dante's Circles		Hemingway's Circles		
Circle #	Sinners	Death Chapter #	Criminals	Corresponds to Dante's
1	(Limbo)	1–6	(Limbo)	(Limbo)
2	The Carnal/ Lustful	7	Decadent Artists	Gluttons
3	The Gluttons	8	The Mean, Misers	Misers
4	The Misers and Spendthrifts	9	Fake Messiahs (including Authors)	Heretics; also, Fraudulent
5	The Wrathful And Sullen	10	The Lustful	Carnal/Lustful
6	The Heretics; Serious Criminals	11	Husbands who lead dangerous lives	
7	The Violent: against others (murderers) against self (suicides) against God (blasphemers) against nature (homosexuals)	12	Literary Critics	Wrathful/Sullen
8	The Fraudulent (Flatterers and Sorcerers)	14	Inpresarios, Other Traitors to Art	Traitors; also, Fraudulent/ Flatterers
9	Traitors	15	Crimes against nature	Violent

After meeting the Old Lady in the first dialogue, in which she emerges from limbo, the narrator takes her to the evocatively named Café Fornos. Although the real Café Fornos was a hangout for bullfighters and aficionados in Madrid (Mandel 147–48), "fornos" suggests not only "fornication" (in Spanish, *fornicar,* or "knowing in the biblical sense," which will accrue additional significance later, when the Old Lady refers to "knowing" the Author), but also, in Italian (*forno*), oven (or hell, or *Inferno*).

The second Author–Old Lady dialogue, at the end of chapter 7 (70–72), identifies the sins of the decadent (or degrading) artist and hinges on the two meanings of "decadence" (philological versus popular). The Old Lady, alluding to *Hamlet,* gives the word its popular meaning: "I always understood it to mean that there was something rotten as there is at courts" (71). The still-unlabeled Author notes that "decadence is a difficult word to use since it has become little more than a term of abuse applied by critics to anything they do not yet understand or which seems to differ from their moral concepts" (70–71). He gives his definition, the philological one, as decay—in this context, "the decay of a complete art through a magnification of certain of its aspects" (70).

In this second dialogue, Hemingway hides his project in plain view. To perceive it, the reader must remember this section more than twenty pages later, when the Author is finally labeled as a character. "Author," like "decadence," is another word that is "difficult to use," one that is "applied by critics" to something they do not understand, especially when they are abusing Hemingway for works that "differ from their moral concepts" (70–71). The stakes of this abuse are "the decay of a complete art through a magnification of certain of its aspects," i.e., the critical magnification of the public author's importance to the detriment of his writing. The Old Lady does this to the Author, to the detriment of the stories he tells her ("A Natural History of the Dead" and the subsequent anecdote about homosexuals in Paris). And Hemingway's critics will do this to him, again, in their reviews of *Death in the Afternoon,* proving his point by missing it completely.

Their third dialogue (82–83) concerns economics: the miserliness of the matadors, who "are . . . miserly slave drivers with those who work for them. . . . There is no man meaner about money with his inferiors than your matador" (82). In these first three Author–Old Lady dialogues, the narrative voice is nearly indistinguishable from that of previous chapters. It delivers much the same information as did the narrator, listing the matadors of the day (70) and (appropriately, if pompously) alluding to the dual connotations of the word "decadence" (71). The same voice will caution the Old Lady against starting "your writer to talking of words" and alert her to the dangers of linguistic ambiguity, since terms "cannot mean the same to all" (71). It is crucial that the identity of the voice also be ambiguous in this early dialogue in order that the distinction may be seen as a process of mutation and decay. By transforming this unnamed didactic voice—what the critics would name "the author"—into the Author character, Hemingway underscores his point that the word "author," like the apt word "decadence," is itself susceptible to multiple meanings, depending on one's perspective.

As the dialogues continue, the Old Lady's presence proves that like a bull-fighter, an author "will not be better than his audience very long" (163). The fourth dialogue (92–95) follows a discussion of "fake messiahs," matadors who are brilliant specialists but are hyped by critics as "gods" (86). This dialogue—which concerns horses' internal organs and sawdust, shrimp, Italian restaurants, and politicians—seems to be random, but what connects these is the power of the gaze to impose meaning, to exaggerate an aspect of reality, thus falsifying its whole: the sawdust-filled horses look healthy, but they are dying; the politicians become statesmen through the transformative power of a watching public; and through the power of the Old Lady's limited perception, the narrator becomes, as promised, the Author. She makes him an authority on just about everything, including the shrimp she sees and wants to try. Once her attention turns entirely away from bullfights and words and she begins to treat the narrator as an authority on "the gentleman smoking the cigar," "those things he is eating," and where to dine (93), the Author is given is new label. The formal presentation of the dialogue now has two labeled characters; it has become the script for a play. The Author responds to the Old Lady's imposition of authority by toying with her, thus isolating "another part" of the now disjunct narrative voice in order that it may remain a sacred space, "completely open to observe and judge" (95).

In this fourth dialogue the Old Lady begins to ask stupid questions ("But surely the horse could not permanently replace those [lost internal] organs with sawdust?" [92]) and to deliver insipid observations ("I find it [that replacement] very cleanly, that is if the sawdust be pure and sweet"—in other words, she tautologically opines that sawdust is clean if it is clean [92]). At this point, the narrator begins to lose patience. Within a page, this exasperation is given its own voice, labeled Author. The narrator will coexist with this newly named voice; which one speaks depends on the Old Lady. Henceforth in the text, the value of her questions determines the tone of the Author's response. When she asks serious questions about bullfighters and bulls, she is answered seriously; when she critiques the narrator or the content of his replies, she is answered, increasingly caustically, by the Author:

Author: Madame, rarely will you meet a more prejudiced man nor one who tells himself he keeps his mind more open. But cannot that be because one part of our mind, that which we act with, becomes prejudiced through experience and still we keep another part completely open to observe and judge with?

Old Lady: Sir, I do not know.

Author: Madame, neither do I and it may well be that we are talking horseshit. (95)

The narrator has become prejudiced through his experience of the Old Lady and becomes the Author in the process. As the narrator responds to her limited perspective, his tone changes from humorous to irascible to sarcastic. Hemingway thus articulates the split between Author, who has become "prejudiced through experience," and writer, whose mind remains "completely open."

When delivering information about bullfighting and writing, the Author is indistinguishable from the original first-person narrator. When the Old Lady asks stupid, random questions, Hemingway labels the Author's lines, thus distinguishing between "I" as narrator and "I" as abstract character, one aspect of whose identity (authority) has been magnified to the elision of the rest. This dialogue ends with the Old Lady's dramatically ironic line "I must learn to use these terms correctly" (95); the term she least understands—that term Hemingway designed her to misunderstand—is "author."

In the remaining dialogues, the now-labeled Author openly plays Virgil to the Old Lady's pilgrim, leading her through a discussion of vices and sins. The fifth and sixth dialogues concern the adulterers and the promiscuous (chap. 10, 103–4; in Dante, the Lustful) and dangerous husbands (chap. 11, 120–123; this sin is, rather appropriately, particular to Hemingway). The dialogue in chapter 12 is more complicated; it initially concerns suicides, thieves, and unscrupulous bull-breeders, all of which refer to items of news stolen from Hemingway's personal life (his father's suicide) and/or criticism of his writing (by unscrupulous "bull" breeders), both sides of his life having become public property since his affair with Pauline Pfeiffer in 1927.

Hemingway reserves the lowest three circles of hell for critics, from whom he felt he must redeem his writing. The seventh dialogue, in chapter 12, although initially about violence to the self, develops into a complex illustration of the wrathful and sullen, first in the allusive story "The Natural History of the Dead" (which in its Dantean structure constitutes a parable, a cross between the Books of Exodus and Job) and in the Old Lady's response to it.

In the story, which the Old Lady has requested and which prefigures (on the micro level) what the narrator (God) will do to the Author and Old Lady (sinners) after the last dialogue, a wounded soldier lies dying at an aid station while an artillery officer berates the doctor in charge for not performing euthanasia. The angry officer tells the doctor, "You are crazy," and accuses him of inhumanity ("I will shoot the poor fellow . . . I am a humane man") (142). The doctor does not defend his humanity; instead, because he must function as the post's God, overseeing not only parts but the whole, he pulls rank on the officer, asking, "Are you in command of this dressing post? Do me the courtesy to answer." The artillery officer becomes first sullen:

> The lieutenant of artillery said nothing . . .
> "Answer me," said the doctor . . ."Give me a response."
> and then wrathful:
> "F—k yourself," said the artillery officer.
> "So," said the doctor. "So, you said that. All right. All right. We shall see."
> The lieutenant of artillery stood up and walked toward him.
> "F—k" yourself," he said. "F—k yourself. F—k your mother. F—k your sister. . . ." (143)

The doctor then blinds the officer, whose wrath increases:

> The doctor tossed the saucer full of iodine in his face. As he came toward him, blinded, the lieutenant fumbled for his pistol. The doctor skipped quickly behind him, tripped him and, as he fell to the floor, kicked him several times and picked up the pistol in his rubber gloves. The lieutenant sat on the floor holding his good hand to his eyes. (143)

In these passages, the artillery lieutenant attempts to function as a self-appointed Moses in his attempt to lead the suffering man out of the captivity of his pain but makes the mistake of looking upon God's face (unlike Moses, who turns his face away from the burning bush in fear [Exodus 3.14]). The doctor then becomes the God of the Old Testament to the lieutenant's uncooperative Moses/voluble Job. He blinds the lieutenant for presuming to challenge his authority; insists, essentially, "I AM THAT I AM" (Exodus 3.14); beats him; and then forgives him for knowing "who's boss" (Job 42.7, 9–10, 12) (which resonates on the macro level of *Death in the Afternoon,* in which Hemingway blinded his critics in hope that they would achieve redemption by comprehending his project). The lieutenant would have done well to heed Virgil's comments in Dante's eighth circle: "Who could be more impious than the one who'd dare sorrow at the judgment God decrees" (20.29–30). Although Hemingway did not map his allusions neatly, the resonances are blatant.

The Old Lady is as blinded by the story's subject matter as the officer is by the iodine (and as the critics would be by Hemingway's reputation as an uncultured anti-intellectual). One would expect such an Old Lady to catch the Biblical allusions, at least, and to understand that the story is a parable, but she merely complains: "I don't care for the title" (133), "This is not amusing" (137), and "Is that the end?" (144). Meanwhile, the Author toys with her, switching blithely from Biblical allusion to mythology: "We aim so high and yet we miss the target"—thus figuring the Old Lady as Icarus. She who has presumed to know the Author, does not know that she cannot know him. She is blind to the quality of this story (which, like all the Author–Old Lady interactions, is exaggerated) and yet presumes, metaphorically, to look upon the Author's face: "You know, I like you less and less the more I know you" (144). She has committed the cardinal sin of critics, confusing the abstract role of authorship (personified as the Author) with a knowable person. But Hemingway insists that authorship reveals no more about the real person behind it than the burning bush reveals about God. Both are only partial reflections of aspects of a whole; what is behind it remains a mystery.

Hemingway's eighth circle (chap. 14) is reserved for art's traitors—impresarios who destroy the art they underwrite; critics who pander; and artists who allow critical attention to sway them from their talent and craft. Hemingway's most stringent assessment of the extent to which critical attention skews audiences away from the real (in the ring or on the page) appears in his discussion of professional matadors and their reliance on biased newspaper reporting. In this chapter, the narrator presents and dismisses the several matadors whose publicity touted them as messiahs, which brought about the diminishment of their art. He reserves his most scathing judgment for Ortega, whose press placed him at the pinnacle of success (168) while those who had seen him fight were wavering between ambivalence and disapprobation (169).

On May 30, Ortega had displayed some good technique, but "the rest of him was ignorance, awkwardness, inability to use his left hand, conceit, and attitudes. He had, very obviously, been reading and believing his own newspaper propaganda" (169). His performances worsened throughout the season, losing what good points he had had, failing to "justify his propaganda," showing signs of cowardice, and finally, in Pamplona, being "so bad he was disgusting" (169). The narrator marks Ortega for condemnation based on his having allowed critical response, which he had paid for, to destroy his merit; the narrator ends by judging him based on the economics of art: "He was being paid twenty-three thousand pesetas a fight and he did absolutely nothing that was not ignorant, vulgar, or low" (170). The narrator spreads his condemnation of the individual, however, to the evil in the system of art production—its critics and its audience. "One of the principal evils of bullfighting in Spain," he continues, is "the fact that because these critics live principally on the money they receive from matadors, their viewpoint is entirely that of the matador" (163). And for an audience member to take the matadors' viewpoint is dangerous to the art, because "you put yourself in the bullfighters' place, put up with their disasters on the bulls they fail with, and wait for the bull they want. Once you do that you become as guilty as any of those that live off and destroy bullfighting and you are more guilty because you are paying to help destroy it" (162). The only recourse is to "know what is good and what is bad, to appreciate the new but let nothing confuse your standards" (162)—especially in making judgments, which should be based on professional performance, not on the man. The lines between person and performance, Hemingway insists, must thus be maintained by all parties: by the professional, lest he believe himself more capable than he is and thus waste his talent; by the critics, lest in their inaccuracy they cause preformed opinion to supercede artistic judgment by performer and audience member; and by the audience, lest in their ignorance and economic power they transform what could be art into mere shallow spectacle.

Death in the Afternoon's analogy between bullfighting and professional writing thus insists that the standards by which to judge an author (the public, professional role) are analogous to those by which one may judge a matador. Writing and bullfighting are actions; author and matador are labels one achieves by performing these actions in public. Such performances require meeting sometimes conflicting criteria, imposed variously by the audience and by the institutional apparatus surrounding any profit-making action.

The Old Lady gets the point of this chapter better than any of the others (perhaps because it is most germane to her role as an audience member). Her accusation that the Author, a bullfight critic who has never been a bullfighter, is a hypocrite evokes Shakespeare's "He jests at scars that never felt a wound" (*Romeo* 2.2.1): "Did they not wound you in horrible fashion? Why are you alive to-day? . . . Were there witnesses to these feats you tell of? Or do you just invent them as a writer?" (171–72). In other words, she condemns him as a fake messiah (which, of course, being the Author and not the author, he is—precisely the same mistake his contemporary reviewers would make, albeit in a very different arena).

Hemingway's ninth and deepest circle goes to the Violent Against Nature—which the Old Lady understands as the "unfortunate people" (i.e., homosexuals; Dante's label is the Perverted) about whom she wants a story. But the last word on this violence is reserved for the narrator, who, in his judgment of the Author and Old Lady, will demonstrate that "violent against nature" refers more pertinently to those who would kill the prophets: literary critics who are themselves novelists and should thus understand the authorship problem well enough to avoid critical hypocrisy.

Immediately after discarding the Author and the Old Lady, the narrator (now back in the first person) turns his attention to the critics. He quotes and replies to a critical piece by Aldous Huxley, "Foreheads Villainous Low," in which Huxley accused Hemingway of "feign[ing] stupidity":

> "In [naming a book by this writer] Mr. H. ventures, once, to name an Old Master. There is a phrase, quite admirably expressive [here Mr. Huxley inserts a compliment], a single phrase, no more, about 'the bitter nail-holes' of Mantegna's Christs; then quickly, quickly, appalled by his own temerity, the author passes on (as Mrs. Gaskell might hastily have passed on, if she had somehow been betrayed into mentioning a water-closet), passes on, shamefacedly, to speak once more of Lower Things.
>
> "There was a time, not so long ago, when the stupid and uneducated aspired to be thought intelligent and cultured. The current of aspiration has changed its direction. It is not at all uncommon now to find intelligent and cultured people doing their best to feign stupidity and to conceal the fact that they have received an education"—and more; more in Mr. Huxley's best educated vein which is a highly educated vein indeed.
>
> What about that, you say? Mr. Huxley scores there, all right, all right. What have you to say to that? (190; brackets in the original)

The narrator proceeds to "answer truly" (190). He insists that authorship is but a performance, a seeming, and that writing is what matters. He begins,

> I believe it is more than a question of the simulation or avoidance of the appearance of culture. When writing a novel a writer should create living people; people not characters. A *character* is a caricature. (191)

As are the Author and Old Lady.

> If a writer can make people live there may be no great characters in his book, but it is possible that his book will remain as a whole; as an entity; as a novel. If the people the writer is making talk of old masters; of music; of modern painting; of letters; or of science then they should talk of those subjects in the novel. If they do not talk of those subjects and the writer makes them talk of them he is a faker, and if he talks about them himself to show how much he knows then he is showing off. (191)

As has the Author.

> No matter how good a phrase or a simile he may have if he puts it in where it is not absolutely necessary and irreplaceable he is spoiling his work for egotism. (191)

As did the Author.

> People in a novel, not skillfully constructed *characters,* must be projected from the writer's assimilated experience, from his knowledge, from his head, from his heart and from all there is of him. If he ever has luck as well as seriousness and gets them out entire they will have more than one dimension and they will last a long time. (191)

Neither the Author nor the Old Lady has more than one dimension; having just been thrown out of the book by the narrator, they will not last—nor, by this logic, should they. "If a writer of prose knows enough about what he is writing about he may omit things that he knows and the reader, if the writer is writing truly enough, will have a feeling of those things as strongly as though the writer had stated them. The dignity of movement of an ice-berg [*sic*] is due to only one-eighth of it being above water" (192). There has been nothing dignified about the Author–Old Lady dialogues; here that is revealed as deliberate. "A writer who omits things because he does not know them only makes hollow places in his writing. A writer who appreciates the seriousness of writing so little that he is anxious to make people see he is formally educated, cultured or well-bred is merely a popinjay" (192). As was the Author, the guise assumed by Hemingway in the construction of the dialogues.

Over the course of the previous nine chapters, Hemingway performed his intelligence and education and cultured status by alluding to and reconstructing morality plays, Dante's *Inferno,* the Sermon on the Mount, *Hamlet, Romeo and Juliet,* and the Books of Exodus and Job, all the while performing trilingual puns, commenting metacritically, and, not incidentally, continuing to deliver detailed information about the art and business of bullfighting. Hemingway has presented his readers with allusion within allegory within analogy within encyclopedia, in nonfiction, fiction, and dramatic genres. He provides Huxley with the performance he had asked for but in its provision reveals its worthlessness. The narrator insists that authorship is but a performance, a seeming, and that writing is what matters, stating essentially, "Mr. Huxley, I know not seems." He deconstructs the Author–Old Lady dialogues in yet another genre switch, this time to literary criticism, turning the tables on Huxley by subjecting Huxley's essay to his own critical scrutiny.

The difference that the narrative voice underscores in Hemingway's "true answer" precisely locates the difference he perceived between the roles of author and writer. Given the choice between "the simulation or avoidance of the appearance of culture" and writing, Hemingway chooses writing. Grammatically, "simulation" and "appearance" are distanced from their verbal actions by nominalization and are doubly distanced by their combination: the "simulation of appearance" is effectively "seeming to seem." Even the literal actions that these words signify ("simulate" and "appear") are static, snapshots of performances (for an implied audience) rather than real actions. Huxley's criticism of Hemingway becomes Hemingway's own criticism—not of Huxley (for that would violate Hemingway's logic) but of Huxley's critique. Through Hemingway's response, the audience perceives Huxley as the performative author while Hemingway emerges, finally, as the writer. In his response to Huxley, Hemingway uses the words "writing" and "writer" twenty-two times, proposing the act of writing as an antidote to Authorial poison. Writing subtly and well was Hemingway's antidote to seeming, and his best revenge against those who would have him seem.

When Gabriel's trumpet sounds in chapter 6, it simultaneously heralds Hemingway's judgment day for his profession and the critics' judgment day for him (and not, as he had desired, for his book). Neither Hemingway nor the critics survived unbloodied. *Death in the Afternoon* was Hemingway's Book of Job, a book designed to even the score between profession and the individual talent, a book in which he took arms against a sea of troubles but, in his opposition, made them worse. For the next eight years, until the 1940 publication of *For Whom the Bell Tolls*, his was a voice crying in the professional wilderness that the right path appeared not anywhere.

Hemingway's metacritical project was understood only vaguely, if at all, by his contemporary critics. These critics missed four crucial points:

1. that the narrator is not the author is not the Author, the Author being a character in *Death in the Afternoon* who constitutes an exaggerated abstraction of professional writing (i.e., critical assumptions regarding authorship and Hemingway);
2. that the Author–Old Lady dialogues generically comprise a morality play about the decadent effects of the publication process on art and its creators;

3. that these dialogues themselves allude (structurally, thematically, and textually) to Dante's *Inferno;* and, thus,

4. that taken together, the Author–Old Lady dialogues present a pilgrim's progress through hell, whereby Hemingway reveals his Author–Old Lady as abstractions and consigns them to purgatory, where they belong.

Whether because his point and his allusions were too subtle, or because his reviewers prejudged him as incapable of either subtlety or allusion, initial critical response to *Death in the Afternoon* confirmed and exacerbated the problem of being "Ernest Hemingway, author." Critics identified two audiences for the book: readers interested in bullfighting and readers interested in Hemingway (Coates 115; Hicks 163; Duffus noted the book's certain appeal to "Hemingway addicts" 113). Despite wondering why Hemingway had written a book on bullfighting (Cowley 120), critics universally accepted him as an authority on that subject. They also accepted him, somewhat grudgingly, as an authority on his own writing, but most seemed baffled as to why he had to thus muddy an otherwise perfectly good book on bullfighting (one critic, Patterson, noted that "the semiautobiographical details" made him "faintly sick" [118]). Cowley and Hicks, at least, realized that Hemingway was deliberately structuring his chapters to underscore the similarities he perceived between the two art forms. But generally, critics who were sharp enough to realize that the book was something more than a tauromachic guide nonetheless floundered in their efforts to identify what that something more was. Granville Hicks, like many others (for example, Duffus 113; Coates 115; Patterson 118; Cowley 121; Mencken 123) concluded it was about the author. When Hicks reviewed *Death in the Afternoon* for the *Nation* in 1932, he wrote that "more people will read the book because they are interested in Hemingway than will . . . because they are interested in bullfighting." He continued: "Fortunately, the author, fully aware of the interest in his personality, has made a vigorous effort to put as much of himself as possible into his book. As a rule, these intimate revelations are placed, for the convenience of the author . . . as well as for the convenience of the reader, at the end of each chapter. At first they take the form of dialogues between the author and an Old Lady . . . Later on . . . the Old Lady disappears, and the author speaks directly to his readers" (163).

Although Hicks noticed the structural and tonal differences between the sections on writing and the Author–Old Lady dialogues, he also missed Hemingway's important distinction. The end-of-chapter dialogues are with the Author, a character, and not with the author, Hemingway. The writer, fully aware of the interest in his personality, had provided a burlesque Hemingway, a windmill for his critics' jousting practice, and he placed them at the end of the chapters because they were a different genre entirely. Distracted by the sweeping red cape of authorship, critics mistook the caricature for the writer behind it.

That distinction is central to Hemingway's project; that distinction is what unifies the book's seemingly disparate genres—the "Baedeker of bulls" (Cowley 121), the essays on writing, the dramatic Author–Old Lady dialogues, and the short story entitled "A Natural History of the Dead." One reviewer, confused by the generic shifts, described his reading experience as feeling "like a chameleon on a patchwork quilt" (Duffus 113). Like his colleagues, he did not see that the parts coalesced into a coherent pedagogical and metacritical project.

The critic whom Hemingway manipulated most effectively with *Death in the Afternoon* was H. L. Mencken, whose review in *American Mercury* applauded the writing in the bullfighting sections even as it missed the pointed institutional critique in the Author–Old Lady dialogues. Mencken identified the Old Lady not as a representation of institutional assumptions regarding readership but as Hemingway's own idea of his readers, and as his perception of some "common denominator of all the Ladies' Aid Societies of his native Oak Park, Ill" (123). Although Hemingway clearly had the "Ladies' Aid" type in mind when he created the Old Lady, and although he was never averse to slighting the "broad lawns and narrow minds" of Oak Park, his motives were more complex. His object was not merely to taunt that element of his readership but to reveal that they were a construction of the publishing industry, of discourses in which critics like Mencken participated. Thus when Mencken missed Hemingway's critique of this assumption, he implicated himself in that very critique. In his conclusion that Hemingway's graphic description of groin goring would "give the Oak Park W.C.T.U. [Women's Christian Temperance Union] another conniption fit," and that "the Hemingway boy is really a case" (124), Mencken committed a spectacular rhetorical error, unwittingly revealing his own implication in the system under Hemingway's scrutiny, committing the very crime Hemingway accused it of.

Neither the Old Lady nor the Author is real; they are abstractions, burlesques of assumptions made by those forces that irresponsibly enact their own authority over art production. *Death in the Afternoon* thus presents, in microcosm, Hemingway's lover's quarrel with his profession. Hemingway chose as the object of his point those purported experts ("authorities") who derived benefit from the economic matrix of art production (indeed, their professional existence depended upon it) but were nonetheless blind to its intrinsic dangers. Hemingway used the book as an opportunity not only to consider critics and their shortcomings but to provide these critics with the opportunity either to overcome or prove these shortcomings, each according to his abilities. Like a skilled matador with a bull, Hemingway metaphorically forced his worst critics to turn in less than their turning radius, using their own momentum and limitations to bring them to their knees. Coming off the popular success of *A Farewell to Arms,* Hemingway did not feel he needed redemption. Nor did his readers. Only his detractors—certain critics—would have argued that redemption was necessary. They, least of all, would be inclined to see *Death in the Afternoon* as redemptive; they, least of all, would take its point. His manipulation of his critics was, however, too subtle. Hemingway had seriously miscalculated his own authority; his reputation, at least, would require more redemption after *Death in the Afternoon* than before it.

His antagonism for his critics was his public response to the problem of being "Ernest Hemingway, author." Knowing that they would comment on "the author" of *Death in the Afternoon,* he readied a straw man, one designed to illustrate and emphasize that an author—like the Author in the book—is a social construct, an economically and discursively defined entity. In *Death in the Afternoon,* Hemingway thus warns his readers not to confuse the author with the man, and, most emphatically, not to trust the judgment of any critic who cannot tell the difference. So warns the Author, in response to Old Lady's criticism that "I like you less and less the more I know you"—"Madame, it is always a mistake to know an author" (144).

Despite the fact that the Author deserves the Old Lady's negative judgment just as thoroughly as she deserves his, it is tempting to assume that Hemingway's sympathies lie entirely with his Author. To do so is to fall into the trap. They lie neither with Author nor Old Lady, but with the writer lying awake at night, trying to remember the "clean, clean, unbearably clean whiteness" of Domingo Hernandorena's thigh bone and its contrast to his dirty underwear. Hemingway's sympathies lie with the writer, with himself as writer, one whose unbearably clean prose would, for the rest of his life, be confused with its author's dirty linen.

In *Death in the Afternoon* he identified the dangers of authorship; its critical reception resulted in his avoiding Personal writing for the better part of the 1930s. But the problem of being "Ernest Hemingway, author," was inescapable and insoluble as long as the writer was also an author, as much a product of the writer writing as the writing itself. The associative logic of Hemingway's Sermon on the Mount project, however pointed, was finally pedagogical. His "blind guide" is his Author, the product of the decadent discourses of authorship and art production—"them which killed the prophets." By his logic, the prophet must be an unmediated dialogue between artist and audience—an ideal Hemingway knew could never be realized. His June 28, 1932, response to Scribner's publicity for *Death in the Afternoon* sums up his assessment of authorship and publishing: "Fuck the whole goddamned lousy racket" (Bruccoli and Trogdon 172).

CHAPTER FIVE

HEMINGWAY'S LOST MANUSCRIPTS

Forty years after his death, Hemingway still has the most recognized face of any American writer, living or dead. His image is used to sell cars, furniture, fountain pens, and, for one brief, lamentable moment, shotguns. His name sells books and keeps people from buying them. It makes people pick his books up and put them down, sometimes reading them in between. He is a marketer's dream and, sometimes, an academic's nightmare. Currently the best place in the world to discuss Hemingway's writing unencumbered by his myth is Cuba, where his celebrity, a product of the United States' economic system, is embargoed.

No one can deny that he courted public attention and had since high school. But if someone had forced him to choose between quality writing and celebrity status, his choice would have been the former. Accepting the Nobel Prize in 1954, he referred to himself insistently as a writer, using the words "writer," "write," and "writing" no fewer than eighteen times in the single-page speech, as he had in response to Huxley in *Death in the Afternoon*.

For Hemingway had long understood that as an author he was as much a product of his typewriter as was his character of the Author. This pleased him even as it angered him; it created opportunities and obstacles. The problems of being "Ernest Hemingway, author," were both enviable and, finally, insoluble. Publication, on which these problems hinge, was for him—and for all writers—both necessary danger and dangerous necessity. As such, he eventually came to understand that publication was and always had been the central problem that informed his writing: specific moments in discretely published stories, relationships of characters in these stories, these stories' relationships to contemporaneously written stories and within chronological series, the series' relationships to each other, and the relationships of paired series to other paired series, all of which form the fractal-like widening gyre whose image introduces this volume.

So I turn again, at the end, to a beginning—not, this time, to an examination of authorship as an extension of writing, but to the beginning of authorship to finally understand a writer.

Hemingway wrote his first letter ever to Maxwell Perkins on April 15, 1925: "I hope someday to have a sort of Daughty's Arabia Deserta of the Bull Ring, a very big book with some wonderful pictures. But one has to save all winter to be able to bum in Spain in the summer and writing classics, I've heard, takes some time. Somehow I don't care about writing a novel and I like to write short stories and I like to work at the bull fight book so I guess I'm a bad prospect for a publisher anyway. Somehow the novel seems to me to be an awfully artificial and worked out form but as some of the short stories are now stretching out to 8,000 to 12,000 words may be I'll get there yet" (quoted in Bruccoli and Trogdon 34).

Two critically acclaimed books of short stories, one critically dismissed satire, two successful novels, the misunderstood bullfight book, a lackluster book of short stories, and a badly received nonfiction safari account later, Hemingway had both proved his early promise and proved himself right—as an author, he had become, by the mid-1930s, a bad prospect for a publisher.

But Perkins had faith in him as a writer. On August 30, 1935, he wrote to Hemingway, saying:

I'm glad you're going to write some stories. All You have to do is to follow your own judgment, or instinct, + disregard what is said . . . When you're ready do a novel. That's what they all must want. That's what they all tell me they want + want me to tell you. I don't think I can tell You anything. If what I have said should worry You + I knew it I'd beg you to disregard + forget it. I can get pretty depressed but even at worst I sill believe—+ its written in all the past—that the utterly real thing in writing is the only thing that counts, + the whole racket melts down before it. All you have to do is trust Yourself. That's the truth.—I say this mostly because I sometimes have thought that You thought I ought to advise You, or keep You advised. I do that for lots of people who write as a trade. With You it seems superfluous + absurd because those things that are important to that kind of writer + affect his fortunes, ought not to have anything to do with You,—+ so far you have not let them. I hope You never will, too. (quoted in Bruccoli and Trogdon 224–25)

But Hemingway did let them. Although his September 7 reply to Perkins's letter asserts, "I will survive this unpopularity and with one more good book of stories (only these are going to be with plenty of action so they can understand them) and one good novel you are in a place where they will all have to come around and eat shit again. I don't give a damn whether I am popular or not" (quoted in Bruccoli and Trogdon 228), for his next book, he capitulated. In 1936, despite the brilliance of his recently published "The Short Happy Life of Francis Macomber" and "The Snows of Kilimanjaro," he gutted his planned book of short stories, stuck two of those stories together ("One Trip Across" and "The Tradesman Returns"), and called the results *To Have and Have Not*—a process he described as lifting "those [two] and finish[ing] this other then with only a couple more stories I have 2 books instead of one and one of them the thing the pricks all love—a novel" (quoted in Bruccoli and Trogdon 244).

With the bullfight book done and his boyhood dream of an African safari realized, he wanted to get back to writing short fiction. His next short fiction, about the Spanish civil war, was primarily journalistic, during the writing of which he got the idea for *For Whom the Bell Tolls*, which would be a major critical and financial success.

After World War II, the pleasure he had had in writing his early short fiction came back to him in the person of Pauline Pfeiffer, who came to visit at the Finca Vigia. Remembering writing this short fiction, he wrote what he remembered about writing it, and he wrote about what he remembered while he was writing it. He also wrote about the writer's desire to write short fiction and about the pressure on the author to publish books. This became *The Garden of Eden,* which stands among other things as Hemingway's memorial to his early short fiction.

When the suitcase containing Hemingway's manuscripts was stolen from Hadley in 1922, he recounted later in *A Moveable Feast,* he wasn't sure he would be able to write again. The first full-length story he wrote after that loss was "Out of Season," which may be the first story he wrote by *remate,* refracting his recent anger at his wife Hadley through memories of a past fishing trip. It is also, however, a rewriting of "Up in Michigan," with the genders switched.

A narrative collation of these two stories reveals that although they evince many superficial differences, they are structurally and thematically the same. They share a kind of skeleton that embraces Hadley Hemingway's loss of the manuscripts in the Gare de Lyon and Hemingway's initial efforts to come to terms with that traumatic experience. Hemingway later reencoded that experience in *The Garden of Eden,* in which Catherine Bourne burns half of the manuscripts her husband David has been writing during their honeymoon. In her efforts to focus David's creative energies on the narrative of that honeymoon, she burns his stories of himself as a child in the wilderness of youth, and of his time spent in the company of his father and his native girlfriend. After the initial shock and white-hot emotions settle, David Bourne is able to rewrite his lost Nick Adams–like stories.

It is safe, and perhaps advisable, to discount the applicability of *The Garden of Eden*'s plot to Hemingway's life, to invoke the phrase "biographical fallacy," and to move on, attributing the scene in which David rewrites his lost stories to self-indulgent, retrospective wish fulfillment on the part of an aging Ernest Hemingway. But if one considers the possibility that the scene in which David rewrites his stories is, like so much else in Hemingway's late fiction, a version of the truth, a startling possibility regarding the lost manuscripts emerges.

Sooner or later, every student of Hemingway's fiction confronts the frustrated desire evoked by the phrase "lost manuscripts." Paul Smith, in his graduate seminar on Hemingway's manuscripts at Trinity College in 1994, tried to appease this frustration by asserting that "the loss of the manuscripts was the best thing that ever happened to Hemingway's writing." In the same seminar, Smith contended that Hemingway's style emerged from the rigorous self-discipline of the "one true sentence" exercises that Hemingway practiced after the loss. Encouraging statements both, but curiosity lingers. What was in those manuscripts? What were those stories about?

A kind of answer to those questions is, finally, suggested if one considers Hemingway as a writer and author. If Jerome McGann's social theory of authorship broadens definitions of "authorship" to include every intervention made by everyone involved in the publication process, from earliest draft to every published version, including those initiated after the death of the writer (*Critique*), then one may broaden his thus implicit definition of "text" to include a text's inception as an prelinguistic idea. By logical extension, then, although the manuscripts themselves were lost and will probably never be recovered, their ideas—their structures, themes, and phrasing, their stories—were not lost at all, nor could they have been, at least to Hemingway. Whether or not Hemingway ever did anything with the stories linguistically inscribed as the lost documents, however, remains to be seen.

McGann's implicit definition of textuality, again broadened to include unwritten ideas, lends validity to the notion that an author's early works may, should specifics so indicate, be considered drafts of later ones, even if the early works saw individual publication and copyright under different titles. This phenomenon is not limited to prose fiction; Beethoven's *Ninth Symphony* builds its "Ode to Joy" movement on a phrase first appearing in his earlier *Choral Fantasy,* and Shakespeare's *The Winter's Tale* reexamines ideas from *Othello* and *The Taming of the Shrew.* Much of Hemingway's early fiction, both draft and published versions, reemerges transformed—indeed, often varied only slightly—in the uncut *The Garden of Eden:* the marriage tales and their complementary Nick Adams stories, his first two novels, and *Death in the Afternoon.* *The Garden of Eden* as written, if not as published, thus figures as Hemingway's textual autobiography, his remembrance of writing past, chronicling in fiction the writer he had been and the writing he had done from the early 1920s through the early 1930s. *The Garden of Eden* is as much about a writer writing as about other themes and issues that have so fruitfully invigorated contemporary Hemingway criticism. A multitextual collation, one that crosses time and genre boundaries, reveals that David's and Andy's creative processes, goals, and texts are identifiably Hemingway's own.

David Bourne's work on his Africa stories and his honeymoon narrative, as well as his stories themselves, maps rather neatly onto the writing of and in the early paired fertility and virility tales. Although publication order obscures the compositional simultaneity of these early paired stories and thus obscures their thematic consanguinity, each pair is thematically linked, examining related aspects of the same questions, questions that were gendered in Hemingway's mind. His broader projects were thus to examine the genders' respective affective and progenerative powers (female fertility and male virility; the female power to create and the male power to transform) and their respective liabilities (the female tendency toward bitchiness and the male's toward apathy; the related female tendency to destroy and—perhaps worse—the male tendency to do nothing at all).

"Out of Season" is a strange tale in these series because it alone of the marriage tales appears to lack a twin fertility story. It alone of the marriage tales privileges the failure of male courage for its narrative affect. It is much more of a virility tale, sharing with the earliest Nick Adams stories both a male protagonist and the representation of a homosocially public failure of male virility. Its companion fertility tale may be found in "Up in Michigan," to which it is virtually identical in terms of structure, situation, and theme.

"Up in Michigan" and "Out of Season" are superficially unrelated: "Up in Michigan" is set in the United States, "Out of Season" in Europe. In "Up in

Michigan," Hemingway transformed people from his adolescence into characters; the point of origin for "Out of Season" is his early adulthood in Italy and Switzerland. Where "Up in Michigan," the story of the loss of Liz Coates's virginity, is overtly sexual, the sexual (or at least procreative) content of "Out of Season" is only implied in the title's reference to spawning season and perhaps to the husband and wife's argument at lunch. The point of view in "Up in Michigan" is that of the protagonist, who is female; the point of view in "Out of Season" is primarily that of the minor character Peduzzi, switching only momentarily to the male protagonist's at key moments in the Concordia and again at the riverbank.

The differences between these stories are many, but their narrative structures and thematic rhetorics match nearly precisely. In many ways, they are exactly the same story, which positions "Out of Season" as a cross-gendered rewriting of "Up in Michigan," one of two extant stories not lost in 1922.

Both stories support the adage "Be careful what you wish for—you might get it," and both end by illustrating the ambivalence that follows hard upon the voluntary surrender of self in the pursuit of pleasure. In "Up in Michigan," Liz Coates wants romance with Jim Gilmore. The young gentleman in "Out of Season" wants to go trout fishing. Both are reasonable wishes, but both are ill judged. The reader, at least, knows that both protagonists are gambling—Liz with her heart and reputation, the young gentleman with the law, and both with their futures. Their fantasies make them easy marks, susceptible to exploitation by drunks; their moral weakness prevents them from leaving, even after they realize that they probably should.

Both stories illustrate a moment that conforms to an insight Hemingway later recorded on the back of the manuscript of "The Doctor and the Doctor's Wife": "When you look back on it you always find a place where you think, well, if I hadn't done that, I'd have been all right" (KL/EH 367, last page verso; Smith, *Guide* 61). In both "Up in Michigan" and "Out of Season," an early failure of courage sets the plots in motion for a downward plunge culminating in a second and irrevocable loss at the stories' climaxes.

Early in "Up in Michigan," Liz wants to make "something special" for Jim to take on his hunting trip, "but she didn't finally because she was afraid to ask Mrs. Smith for the eggs and flour and afraid if she bought them Mrs. Smith would catch her cooking. It would have been all right with Mrs. Smith but Liz was afraid" (82). In the beginning of "Out of Season," the young gentleman asks Peduzzi, "Should his wife come behind with the rods?" (173) Peduzzi confirms that this would be a good idea, thus the young gentleman passes off the visual evidence of lawbreaking to his wife, Tiny. Within a paragraph, Peduzzi, not the young gentleman, feels a twinge of conscience and calls Tiny forward to walk with them, rather than behind. She does not—perhaps because she does not understand him; perhaps because she is angry—and her husband, decidedly no longer a gentleman, shouts at her.

Mrs. Smith and Tiny are the moral compasses in these stories. If Mrs. Smith knew about Liz's infatuation with Jim, she might provide advice, a warning, or closer supervision; she might by her mere presence embarrass Liz into retiring early rather than waiting up for Jim. If the young gentleman had the courage to commit himself fully to lawbreaking, he would not be vulnerable to Tiny's later charge of cowardice: "Of course you haven't got the guts to just go back. . . . Of course you have to go on. . . . I'm going to stay with you. If you go to jail we might as well both go" (176). Tiny has the courage that her husband and Liz Coates lack.

The protagonists' cowardice literally leads them both downhill to sit by the water with a drunken man after their moral compasses withdraw, both compasses walking upward, two-thirds of the way through the stories—at exactly the same moment in the narrative pace. Most striking in terms of the stories' similarities is that down by the water, both protagonists surrender their identities to the drunks in whose hands they have chosen to remain.

The first draft of "Up in Michigan" begins "Fraley Dilworth got the dimple on his chin from his mother. Her name had been Liz Buell. Jim Dilworth married her when he came to Horton's Bay from Canada" (KL/EH 800, 1). Although the published version omits Liz's pregnancy, in Hemingway's mind, at least, Liz's encounter with Jim will result in a child, a marriage, and a name change. Wanting romance, the sentimental phantasm she has constructed from reading Mrs. Gaskell's novels, Liz gets instead dispassionate, fumbling sex, which makes her first "frightened," then "uncomfortable and cramped" (85) . Consequent to this objectively banal moment, Liz will have to choose between the labels of "Liz Coates, whore" and "Liz Gilmore, wife and mother." She surrenders "Liz Coates . . . the neatest girl [Mrs. Smith] had ever seen" (81), and in a multilayered pun, she surrenders her coat to Jim, tucking it around him "neatly and carefully," both kissing him and crying, walking away from him and returning to his side before walking uphill alone (86).

"Out of Season" progresses in the same way. The young gentleman wants fly-fishing; Peduzzi expects country-style worm-and-hook fishing. The young gentleman expects to break the law by fishing out of season but ends up only drinking. Initially committing himself to staying with Peduzzi on the riverbank, he, like Liz, feels "uncomfortable and afraid" (177). And he too will change his status and name, always given from Peduzzi's point of view, from the hierarchical, class-based "gentleman" to the "caro" of equals and friends (178). This story also ends with ambivalence: the young man first pays Peduzzi for the next day's excursion then recants and waffles: "I may not be going. . . . I may not be going . . . very probably not" (179).

Both stories trace the downward trajectory initiated by self-seduction, the cowardly subordination of better judgment to silence, and the subjection of character to public censure. Both stories end with the ambivalence that immediately follows the loss of self, the loss of status, the loss of a name: "If I hadn't done that, I'd have been all right," still recognized myself in the mirror, in the eyes of my wife or my community, still been at home in my own skin. In "Up in Michigan," this is represented by the "coat" pun; in "Out of Season," in the more complex, ever-more ironic shifts from "young gentleman" to "caro" and back. So despite Hemingway's narrative repetition in building and regendering "Out of Season" on the skeletal structure of "Up in Michigan," Smith's assertion that the loss of the manuscripts was a good thing for Hemingway's writing seems to hold true.

Artistic repetition need not be reductive or the sign of a failing writer when that repetition involves enriching transformation and represents the evolution of central, deeply personal, and humanist concerns: What does it mean to be a man, a woman, alone, together, a son, lover, husband, father, and/or writer?

As a writer, Hemingway came as close as he could to becoming a woman as he understood the concept—in nurturing the germ of an idea from conception through insight through creation through publication, working inimitable but discernable transformations on his stories at each step in their growth. Given his maternal relationship to his stories, and the frequency with which he reworked his earlier works into later ones, it seems extremely unlikely that he would—or could—give up the stories in the stolen manuscripts for lost.

Smith called 1924 a "miraculous year" for Hemingway's short fiction. Between the end of February and April of that year, Hemingway completed half of the sixteen full-length stories in the New York *In Our Time*—eight stories that rank among his finest: "Indian Camp," "Cat in the Rain," "The End of Something," "The Three-Day Blow," "The Doctor and the Doctor's Wife," "Mr. and Mrs. Elliot," and "Cross-Country Snow." Smith notes that at least one of these stories, "The Three-Day Blow," may have been a rewriting of a lost manuscript: "In *A Moveable Feast*, Hemingway remembered writing [the] sequel to 'The End of Something' ['The Three-Day Blow'] in January,

1922 (5). Either his memory failed him and he confused two periods of writing . . . or it did not" (Smith, *Guide* 50).

"It is conceivable," Smith continues, based on the kinds of paper that he used and the unusual lack of a handwritten manuscript preceding the typescript one, "that 'The Three-Day Blow' *was* begun in early 1922 and lost with those stolen in December" (50).

If "The Three-Day Blow," then why not others? Why not the earliest Nick Adams stories, perhaps begun as a single novel or Ur-text from which the short stories as eventually published evolved? Using these lost stories to propel the earliest Nick Adams stories, and these stories in male counterpoint to the simultaneously finished marriage-fertility tales is, first, consistent with Hemingway's late creative process; and second, consistent with David Bourne's creative process as depicted in *The Garden of Eden;* and third, may illuminate how Hemingway was able to produce so many works of such sophistication and lasting critical merit in so short a period of time.

This was the time to which Hemingway returned in writing *The Garden of Eden,* the portrait of a young writer at the height of his talent, writing works in pairs: the first, the story of a marriage in which (this time) female fertility fails, and the second, in which (this time) male virility does not fail, stories of a boyhood spent in the company of an outdoorsman father. David Bourne's Nick Adams–like stories are his attempt to escape the complexity of his gendered relationship, but he comes to comprehend the stories' relationship to recent events in his marriage. He tells himself to "use the sorrow you have now to make you know how the early sorrow" felt (and, presumably, vice versa). The closer he writes himself to the live elephant, whose commitment to its dead partner will betray it and kill it, the closer he comes to understanding his wife, whose lack of commitment to his writing betrays and very nearly kills it. David rejects that wife for the more traditional Marita, who commits fully to David's writing, calling it a *mystère; The Garden of Eden* is thus, for all its sexual experimentation, a profoundly conservative novel.

Catherine's burning of David's manuscripts, which he has kept in a suitcase, is so resonant with Hadley's loss of Ernest Hemingway's valise of manuscripts that one need scarcely belabor it. But contents and consequences bear consideration. Catherine burns only the Nick Adams–like Africa stories, and David, after his initial fury has passed and after he has in all probability impregnated Marita, is able to rewrite these stories, only better. Perhaps Hemingway did something similar, improving on the lost stories after the birth of his son in 1923. Indeed, he had the ability to rework earlier stories while improving them—transforming them—as he did with "Up in Michigan" and "Out of Season" in 1923, and again, in the 1940s and 1950s, when he returned to the bones of the early fertility-virility pairs, transforming them into *The Garden of Eden.*

One final question: Why rewrite a story you already have? "Up in Michigan" was not, after all, lost with the others at the Gare de Lyon; it had gotten stuck in a drawer and thus escaped Hadley's notice while she was packing. However, Hemingway thought it was no more publishable than the ones he had lost, and in 1923, that reason still held true. Although it would later see limited circulation among the literary elite in modernist Paris in *Three Stories and Ten Poems,* it would not see widespread corporate publication in the United States until 1938.

The evidence that the lost manuscripts reappear in these 1924 stories is only slim if one insists on a near-verbatim rewriting. If one allows for a broader definition of "rewriting," one that admits thematic and narrative structure as integral to writing, and one consistent with Hemingway's lifelong creative process, the time for wistfulness and frustrated desire is past. It is not only possible but probable that Hemingway's lost stories have already been found, by Hemingway himself.

APPENDIX

THE PROBLEM OF AUTHORSHIP AND TEXTUALITY

In *The Death and Return of the Author,* Sean Burke argues that a close reading of Barthes's "The Death of the Author," Derrida's *Of Grammatology,* and Foucault's "What Is an Author?" reveals that "the concept of the author is never more alive than when being pronounced dead" (7). In the preface to the second edition, Burke responds to charges of negativism by postulating that a positive theory of authorship requires a model that would situate an embodied authorial subjectivity (ix). He suggests several areas that may contribute to such theorization, including copyright (viii), "intellectual ownership" (viii), "the ethics of authorship, the question of legacy and the contractual nature of the signature" (ix).

Responding later to the work of Jerome McGann, he indicates, obliquely, that conceptions of authorship may also be addressed by textual theory: "In saying that 'the critic places himself in a position from which he can treat the literary work as if it were a timeless object, unconnected with history [the position that McGann critiques],' Jerome McGann fails to recognise that such idealisation arises from a lack rather than excess of attention paid to its historical author" (203).

McGann's so-called social theory of textual transmission, established in *A Critique of Modern Textual Criticism* and elaborated in *The Beauty of Inflections* (from which Burke quotes here) reconsiders models of textual criticism and decentralizes the author (or, more accurately, authorial intent). On the surface, this decentralization would seem to support Burke's conclusion that McGann unwarily affirms the definition of authorship he intends to critique. However, McGann's work (which is so often misread as to constitute very nearly a field of study on its own) argues for a broader understanding of the role of the author as one of many nodes within the network of relationships involved in textual production. As such, McGann's model deliberately (rather than accidentally) places a greater burden on authorship than those espoused within the Fredson Bowers–G. Thomas Tanselle tradition of textual criticism. Like many of McGann's detractors, Burke misapplies McGann's social theory to support his own belief that efforts to erase questions of authorship tend to backfire. But McGann's theory, as he himself has stated, does not attempt to erase the author; rather, it restores to authorship its intrinsic social context. Within textual studies, this restoration allows other factors to affect editorial decisions regarding which text, among many, to use as copy-text (that is, as the basis for a new edition) (McGann, *Critique* 203).

Burke's gesture toward textual theory as relevant (but not necessarily vital) to a revised conceptualization of authorship has merits beyond any he implies. McGann's is a distinctive but not representative voice within the discourse; there are those who oppose McGann (among them, those working within the Bowers-Tanselle tradition) and who may contribute much to the project of revision. The discourse of textual theory, which is remarkably (and unnecessarily) divided, has much to offer critical theory in such a reenvisioning. Even the division within the discourse may prove illuminating. Burke's misreading of McGann shares with the Bowers–Tanselle versus McGann schism a problem of inadequate terminology. Although both frequently reference the author, their definitions do not coincide. "Author" and "author" cannot be synonymous when the first signifies an embodied subjectivity (i.e., writer/individual/identity) while the second refers to a discursive node (i.e., author/social role). The Bowers-Tanselle approach to editing, which, generally speaking, attempts to establish authorial intention, tends to focus its attention on the former; McGann argues that one may—but does not necessarily need to—privilege the latter.

The model toward which Burke gestures in his preface, that of the situated and embodied authorial subjectivity, may not reside as far in the future as he fears. This model is immanent in the interstices of current textual theory, philosophical and cultural questions (or denials) of authorship, and recent copyright legislation (the Copyright Term Extension Act of 1998, which modifies Title 17, U.S. Code). By proposing the conjunction of these three discourses, I intend to locate this embodied authorial subjectivity by recovering for critical, theoretical, and textual discourse the figure who has been missing from, but implied by, all of them. Unless I am sorely mistaken, Burke's situated embodiment of authorial subjectivity resides in the figure of the writer, an identity that is separate and distinct from the author.

Although "writer" and "author" refer somewhat confusingly to the same person, a critical distinction between the two is not only desirable but also crucial to considerations of authorship, especially in the area of textual studies concerned with modernist texts. Distinguishing between the writer and the author allows for inquiry at a broader and more clearly identified nexus of critical biography and textual criticism than that addressed (if at all) by current textual theory. At this nexus, the writer is distinguished from the author by virtue of chronological anteriority in the process of textual production (i.e., before the social roles of authorship, including that of copyright holder, come into play). Under refined focus, the writer, a figure all but obscured by its assumed synonymy with the author in socially oriented discourses, can reemerge as an important (not omnipotent or panoptical, but important) figure in the production of textual meaning.

Because of the recent Copyright Term Extension Act, and because of the corporate economic forces behind it, textual scholars working with modernist literature must confront copyright with a skepticism that goes beyond objecting to it as a hindrance. Barred by this piece of legislation from producing critical or scholarly editions for at least twenty years, such scholars must develop new approaches to and methodologies for textual inquiry into works of this period.

In response to this challenge, I have employed the contextual approach I outlined above, which presents the narrative of the writer and the words in the moment of writing. The textual elements of this narrative are usually contained within the textual apparatuses of scholarly editions (specifically, genetic editions), which, if complete, "record but also re-create the development of an idea in an author's mind as well as on the printed page" (Boydston 10). Jo Ann Boydston, in her presidential address to the Society for Textual Scholarship, rightly asserts that "every apparatus has a story to tell that is . . . a story of suspense and discovery, a true textual drama" (10).

Unfortunately (from a pedagogical perspective), relatively few readers pierce the daunting (and somewhat arcane) tabulative form of the apparatus in order to reconstruct that drama for themselves. For this reason, and for reasons of copyright, I have not produced a companion volume containing only textual apparatus and commentary (such a volume would be useful and may be a future project). Although such a volume might constitute a viable alternative to the (currently impossible) production of a critical edition of Hemingway, similar volumes (notably, Matthew Bruccoli's *Apparatus for F. Scott Fitzgerald's* The Great Gatsby) have been, as James West notes, "received indifferently."[1] West continues, "Scholars have now come to realize that if reedited texts are to win acceptance, they must be presented in editions of the actual text, published together with some form of commentary and apparatus" (366). West's description of the copyright situation as leading to this imperative thus leaves the discipline contingent on the permission (or even patronage) of individual literary estates, but this condition only applies if the end product is to be a reedited text. A narrative elaboration of the evolution of a text in the mind of the writer, and a concurrent critical examination of the ways in which circumstances of production contribute to textual meaning, will provide an alternative and accessible approach to inform readers (and readings) of Hemingway's works. These works have their own "textual dramas," their own stories.

From such legislatively imposed compromises comes the opportunity to discover how individual writers addressed the problems of their plural roles (for although "writer" may constitute an identity, "author" is a role, as I discuss in chapter 4). Collation (the comparison of multiple versions of texts) performed without the imperative to produce an edition allows the relationships between a writer and his or her text(s) to emerge as dynamic, rather than static. For Hemingway, both the act and the product of writing constituted a site for identity construction; as such, investigating these relationships reveals a growing tension between writer and author and their often contradictory definitions of text(s) and textuality. I employ the materials of textual inquiry—manuscripts, typescripts, galleys, and published versions—as the primary site at which to consider Hemingway's own interrogation of his métier and his profession, but having been freed by copyright from restricting my inquiry to a discrete portion of the text, I can consider multiple texts simultaneously.

Since textuality and identity were congruent for Hemingway, consideration of that interrelationship over a period of time reveals a fluid subjectivity that responds variously to many stimuli, including the problems of intrinsically social authorship and publication. Understanding this fluidity at various points in his career and in relation to specific texts (and textuality) allows for greater nuance in our understanding of both text(s) and writer.[2]

Problems of the Text(s) and Textuality

However complex the political and philosophical ramifications of recent copyright legislation, its impact on the field of twentieth-century textual studies, and Hemingway studies in particular, is clear: readers' access to Hemingway's works is unfortunately limited to currently available editions. These editions are demonstrably flawed and uniformly deceptive. Never mind what Hemingway intended; readers who lack specialized knowledge and access to multiple geographically scattered collections do not—and, worse, cannot—know what Hemingway wrote. This situation will persist until 2020, the earliest year in which the first of Hemingway's published works may enter the public domain.

When the current standard editions of his short fiction are collated against earlier versions, numerous substantive variants emerge. These variants affect and effect meaning; by their very nature they tend to be invisible to the vast majority of Hemingway's readers. Equally problematic is the status of Hemingway's posthumously published works (to date: *A Moveable Feast, Islands in the Stream,* "The Last Good Country," *The Dangerous Summer, The Garden of Eden,* and *True at First Light*). Each of these works has been edited (most often, cut), in some cases heavily and in all nearly invisibly. Should a reader think to question the status (or even the words) of the available texts—and there are no warning flags that would alert a general reader to do so—the volumes themselves contain neither answers nor the means by which to begin to find them.

It is a maxim of the book trade that there is no such thing as a perfect book. According to this maxim, every book has at least one mistake in it, varying in degree from typographical errors to sections that, through printer error, are missing completely. Such errors are easily located by most readers. But every commercially printed text is subject to the interventions of multiple individuals during its transformation from manuscript to published form, resulting in other kinds of linguistic changes. Whereas alterations made during this process do not necessarily constitute mistakes, readers may want (or even need) some indication that these alterations have occurred, a clear identification of what they are, and perhaps an account of their history. In the absence of a textual apparatus (the component of the critical edition whereby such information is provided) or a visit to the physical archive (should such be feasible), readers of many modernist works lack crucial information, the likes of which are available to the readers of earlier works merely at the turn of a page.

The dissemination of such information in its traditional format, the critical edition, has been proscribed by Congress in an effort to secure copyrightable material against unauthorized economic exploitation. One pragmatic definition of the author, based upon current legal discourse, then, might read "the institution that controls access to copyrighted material." By this definition, the author is anything but dead: he has been legally granted a temporary stay of mortality. He is favored among individual citizens in that after death, he legally retains his ability to earn income.

On the surface, there should be little reason to question the rights of an individual to provide for heirs. As becomes evident after even a brief reflection on copyright, however, a professional writer of works in copyright inhabits and proposes at least a dual identity. One objective of my project will therefore be to investigate the multifaceted nature of this authorial identity, not in an attempt to reconcile the various definitions of authorship advocated in current legal, cultural, and textual discourses, but, rather, in order to distinguish from these multiple discourses one aspect of the textual process that is currently obscured and/or elided by them all, one that needs to be restored specifically to the discourse of textual theory and criticism.

Textual theory largely blurs the critical distinction between the writer (the person who writes the text) and the author (the person whose text is published) that is implicit under copyright law. By far the most vigorous and long-standing debate among textual theorists concerns the concept of authorial intention and its importance in the choice of privileging copy-text or base text (the text on which to base a critical edition). This debate, very generally speaking, asks two questions: whether or not one can ascertain authorial intention, and whether or not one is obligated to try.

What is implicit in this debate is the assumption that there is a distinct and universally understood boundary between archival material and material in public circulation, and the related question of whether or not something happens to texts at that boundary. Jerome McGann's extended inquiry into what that something is allows for a much broader definition of the archive than is usually assumed: that the archive should include not only manuscripts, typescripts, proofs, and early editions but also all the subsequent events (or editions) that, taken together, comprise the work's historical identity ("What Is" 24). But even in this inclusive definition, the boundary between archive and public remains a constitutive force in how textual scholars think about specific texts. McGann argues that between the private (the more traditional definition of the archive) and the public (which evokes the literal connotation of "publication") there lies a complex of social and institutional relationships, all of which can affect the linguistic and bibliographic codes that, taken together, constitute what we commonly call the text. Thus McGann's theory of textual transmission asserts the necessity of inquiry at and into the boundary but takes the boundary itself, however wide, as an assumption.

Even in McGann's argument that one need not automatically (i.e., uncritically) locate one's choice of copy-text by virtue of its chronological proximity to that boundary, the text is nonetheless assumed to change its status in some ineffable and permanent way when it enters into the processes that occur there. In current textual theory this boundary functions as the site for the loss of a kind of textual virginity which, once lost, is irrecoverable. Its status in the perceptions of the writer and author, however, may be markedly different from that forwarded by theory, and may affect textual meanings and the meaning of textuality.

When the point of textual inquiry is to produce a critical edition, this boundary is of central importance to questions governing the selection of copy-text. Such questions, and the theoretical debate that addresses them, seek to resolve issues of authorial intention and its relevance to editors and editorial methodologies. In situations in which the production of a critical edition is legally inadvisable, however, as in the case of Hemingway's works, questions governing the selection of copy-text lose their centrality. Others emerge, the presence of which has been obscured by the copy-text debate, and asking these questions may broaden and perhaps realign current critical understandings of such fundamental concepts as textuality and authorship.

I contend that there are two concurrent (and related) and relatively untheorized changes of status that occur at that boundary. The first concerns the identity of the person who originally wrote the text in question. Textual discourse today uncritically but implicitly asserts that, at this boundary, the writer assumes an additional identity, one that is public, social, institutional, cultural, and legal—at this boundary, the writer becomes, additionally, an author. The second change, which is idiosyncratic and as such must be assessed case by case, concerns the relationships of a particular writer both to the text, which is no longer exclusively his, and to the author that he has become.

Lamentably, and perhaps because textual scholarship must work chronologically backward to ascertain lines of textual transmission, theories of textuality and textual scholarship tend implicitly to extend the role of authorship backward as well, past that boundary, into the writer's space of initial creation (which, to the extent that the mind is a private place, occurs in private). Because of the lack of critical distinctions between author and writer, textual scholars may grant authorship a province which it does not, and should not (by its own definition) warrant. "Authorship" in current discourse identifies not merely a practice but an identity, and, within the related context of copyright law, a static one. It seems tautological to say that once one authors a text; one cannot write it. But "author" does not equal "authorize," and authorization can in any case be revoked (as, for example, Yeats was fond of doing [Bornstein, "Remaking"]). Between the fact of copyright and the literal definition of the word "publication" (to make public), this presumed identity seems both fundamental and irrevocable. Its guise serves social constructivist arguments regarding the production of texts, literature, and art but obscures (or erases) the relationship of the individual writer to his texts and to his authorial role.

Any role that achieves the status of an innate identity on the basis of linguistics and the legal system must be subjected to critical interrogation, however. Such scrutiny makes evident that this identity obscures as much about what it purports to reveal—the writer—as it reveals about the social institutions it effectively erases—those institutions by whose auspices writing reaches the public. The assumption that authorial identity supersedes or replaces altogether that of the writer runs counter to the writer's own perception. While becoming a published author may be the professional status to which writers aspire, authorship itself becomes a site of struggle for writers who enact their subjectivity by and in their writing. In those cases, authorship and questions of authorship become integral to that writing. Over the course of a writing life (and the course of a career, which although concurrent, begins, necessarily, somewhat after one begins to write), writership and authorship must necessarily coexist in a dynamic, rather than static, tension.

NOTES

Introduction: The Hemingway Text

1. Paul Smith dispels the "Peduzzi myth" with evidence from Hemingway's biography and his manuscripts. He concludes, "If the original of Peduzzi ever existed, he may have done himself in sometime between the spring of 1923 and December of 1925 but not in time to immortalize himself as the donné of Hemingway's first theory" (*Guide* 20).

2. For an excellent assessment of contemporary critical response to Hemingway in the 1930s, see Lionel Trilling's 1939 review of *The Fifth Column and the First Forty-Nine Stories* in *Partisan Review.* Trilling notes that this decade divided Hemingway into "the artist" and "the man" and excused or reviled one's failures in defense or exaltation of the other (279–80).

The Personal Stories I (Paris, 1923–1925)

1. Except in the rare instances where it is otherwise noted, all dates of biographical events are from Michael S. Reynolds' five-volume biography. Likewise, composition dates for Hemingway's short fiction given here and elsewhere in the text come from Smith's *A Reader's Guide to the Short Stories of Ernest Hemingway.*

2. Although it is difficult to imagine two more different writers, stylistically, their writerly projects of retrieving, or refinding, "lost" time are strikingly similar. In 1934, he asked Maxwell Perkins "to send him the '4 volume Proust'" (Burwell 187n). Burwell writes, "By 1953, *remembrance of things past* had become shorthand for Hemingway's writing about his early years, and mentions of Proust in correspondence with Buck Lanham indicate that he was rereading him. He also complains to Wallace Meyer, his Scribner's editor, that the 'literary detectives' (at this point Philip Young and Charles Fenton) who want to probe into his past 'destroy all possibility of your own Remembrance of Things Past where Albertine was really a girl and not your chauffeur'" (187n). Just before his death in 1961, he remarked that "rightly or wrongly all remembrance of things past is fiction" (file 122; quoted in Burwell 188n), echoing his much earlier assertion that "Memory is never true" (*Death* 100).

3. See, for example, Spilka (*Quarrel*), Comley and Scholes, and Moddelmog.

4. His first published works appeared only in Paris; the first fiction work to appear in the United States was "My Old Man," which was published in Edward J. O'Brien's annual *Best Short Stories of 1923* (released in 1924). *In Our Time* was the first Hemingway book to be published in the United States (by Boni & Liveright); it was released in 1925. (See Hanneman 5–7 for his first books and 91 for his contribution to O'Brien's volume.)

5. Smith states that the marriage tales "portray a rootless, wandering couple miserably mismatched" (*Guide* 161) and chronicle the breakdown of Hemingway's first marriage (82).

6. See introduction, note 1. Not all the Nick Adams stories meet Hemingway's experiential criterion for inclusion in the Personal category. Nick is one of the protagonists in "The Killers," for example, but this story was apparently created entirely from imagination rather than the transformation of personal experience.

7. A third problem would later develop from these two early ones: the tension between his emotional dependence on writing and his financial (and, later, psychological) dependence on publication.

8. Kenneth Johnston has suggested that their problems are indicated, metaphorically, by the story's title—fishing is illegal in spawning season. Johnston combines this lawbreaking with the wife's petulance and the husband's impatience to conclude that the couple in the story is therefore expecting a child and is unhappy about it. However, the wife need not be pregnant for the story to work.

9. As an intimate of the circle at Sylvia Beach's Shakespeare and Company, Hemingway would have witnessed firsthand the extreme financial duress of James Joyce's family. Beach, who was in the process of publishing *Ulysses* when the Hemingways arrived in Paris, had been generously supporting Joyce, his wife Nora, and their children, although she was often barely able to meet her operating costs in order to provide Joyce with what she kindly termed "advances" (see Fitch as well as Beach).

10. In "The End of Something" and "The Three-Day Blow," Hemingway's implied sympathy and respect extend to Nick's girlfriend, Marjorie. Marjorie does not, however, constitute the affective focus of either story; Nick's emotions do. This pattern also holds true however one interprets the ambiguities in "Hills Like White Elephants." Should even the worst happen, should the American man convince his lover, Jig, to undergo an abortion that she clearly does not want, the reader will blame the man and cast his or her sympathy with Jig. In the next chapter, I will argue the possibility of a much less malign interpretation of the story, one in which Jig and her unborn child narrowly escape victimization and in which the man realizes his own culpability. In this interpretation, the man's realization and subsequent resolve qualify him for his share of sympathy as well.

11. See Pamela Smiley, who analyzes the dialogue in "Hills Like White Elephants" and concludes that this miscommunication is the couple's problem. As will be discussed in chapter 2, a variant reading suggests instead that gendered miscommunication exacerbates a different, underlying, nameless problem.

12. Betty Friedan describes "the problem that has no name" in *The Feminine Mystique*. This nameless problem may manifest itself as boredom, infantilization, dissatisfaction with a spouse, and petulance. Beneath such surface manifestations, Friedan argues, there lies a social and cultural epidemic that wastes the potential and talent of women. Although Friedan's investigation is specific to women of a certain class and education level in the postwar 1950s, the wife in Hemingway's "Cat in the Rain" manifests similar

symptoms. Although the period is different, the symptoms are the same: she needs something to do but has no tools to identify what that might be. Even if her wants were to be satisfied, it is likely that the problem would persist.

13. Even in his earliest surviving story (excepting the juvenilia), "Up in Michigan," he writes of Liz Coates's loss of virginity from the woman's perspective, evoking a complex of conflicting emotions, from curiosity to desire to fear to tenderness, without trivializing or softening any of them.

14. This is an eerie moment, biographically; Hemingway's father, Dr. Clarence ("Ed") Hemingway would commit suicide by gunshot in his bedroom five years later.

15. Among Hemingway's nicknames for Hadley were "Cat" and "Feather-kitty." For an in-depth discussion of the associations between cats and women in Hemingway's life and fiction, see Eby (chap. 4, esp p. 121–25).

16. In the current filing system at the John F. Kennedy Library, the last three pages of the first draft are filed separately and are incorrectly identified by Smith as a rejected insertion of the story (*Guide* 81). The first incomplete draft of the story is thus contained in file 344, pp. 1–5, and file 345, pp. 6–8; the rest of file 345 constitutes a second draft of pp. 6–8 and a first draft of the remaining pages.

17. This image is the one most often cited by critics, especially Warren Bennett, as the proof that the wife in "Cat in the Rain" wants a baby; as the final image in the story, it leads them to conclude that the baby issue is the key to the story.

The Personal Stories II (Paris and Provence, 1926–1927)

1. These subtleties are now discernable to general readers in part because of the opening of archival materials, which in 1926 were, of course, still private.

2. Kennedy's discussion of the "displacement of emotional content onto fictive terrain" in *Imagining Paris* refers specifically to Hemingway's writing of *The Sun Also Rises*. This displacement, however, figures centrally in much, if not all, of Hemingway's fiction writing. Kennedy refers here to Hemingway's own practice, but Hemingway's first-person narrators often perform the same displacement that Hemingway does (especially in the early fiction, as here, in "A Canary for One"). This is but one of many reasons why it is often difficult to separate Hemingway's characters (especially his narrators) from Hemingway himself. As Jackson Benson notes in an early assessment of Hemingway criticism, "many of us in Hemingway studies have trod very close to the line of biographical fallacy. It is a temptation that comes out of the nature of the material itself: if a writer chooses to use his own name as the name of the central character in the early drafts of his fiction [NB: Hemingway did this once], if he models his characters very closely after his own family and friends, and if he appears to be using his writing, often in very direct ways, as a tool to expiate the ghosts and goblins of his own psyche, then the critic is almost inevitably involved in some very sticky critical problems" (32–33). Benson illustrates his point by citing Bertram Sarason, who "met some resistance" from some of the "characters" (not people) he attempted to interview for his work on *The Sun Also Rises* (33).

3. Readers familiar with Hemingway's biography know that Pauline did, in fact, return to marry Ernest; it is thus easy to forget that Hemingway himself did not yet know this and as such to read the story as concerned exclusively with Ernest and Hadley and

not as a representation of his fear of losing both women. In the fall of 1926, double loss was still a possible outcome.

4. The "story of the story" is not without its own irony: six days after Scribner's accepted the story, Hadley agreed to divorce and Hemingway immediately cabled Pauline to join him in Paris.

5. Unlike the "burning house" section, as it was finally published, the "wrecked cars" passage, which occurs near the end of the story, appears in its own two-sentence paragraph for greater impact.

6. Gerald and his wife Sara, upon whom Fitzgerald would loosely base the Divers in *Tender Is the Night*, were friendly with Fitzgerald and Picasso; Picasso was an intimate of Gertrude Stein's; and all were connected with Sylvia Beach, who was Joyce's publisher and well known throughout literary Paris. Secrets among the tightly knit group of literary expatriates in Paris must have been very difficult, if not impossible, to keep. (See Vaill.)

7. Although he never set a story there, Oak Park figures centrally in much of what he wrote. In his Christmas letter to his parents that year, he carefully avoided mentioning the separation from Hadley, although he knew by that time that the marriage was over—Hadley would soon initiate divorce proceedings on the grounds of desertion—and that Pauline was coming back to France to marry him.

8. The lines also prefigure the Switzerland idyll, during which Frederic and Catherine await the birth of their child in *A Farewell to Arms*.

9. For the complete narrative of Scott and Zelda's difficult courtship, see Milford (24–62) and especially Bryer and Barks.

10. At this time, Gerald Murphy had deposited a loan into Hemingway's account; Hemingway had promised *The Sun Also Rises* royalties to Hadley (Reynolds, *Homecoming* 58, 91; Reynolds, *Chronology* 47).

11. See Kennedy (chap. 3) for an excellent summary and critical assessment of this alienation and how it manifested in Hemingway's psyche and writing.

12. In his consideration of the drafts of this story, Donaldson ("Preparing") argues convincingly that the ending is not a surprise, as previous critics had argued, but rather is carefully foreshadowed by the various images in the story.

13. Hemingway would overtly identify this anxiety in a later story, "The Sea Change" (published in 1933), although in that story the character's anxiety is not about the effect of publication on himself (for Hemingway, that would come much later) but about the effect of his writing on his romantic relationships. Hemingway seems to have consciously realized this sometime between "A Canary for One" and "The Sea Change," probably after his friends' reactions to their appearing as recognizable characters (in fictional situations) in *The Sun Also Rises* made the obvious dangers of his Personal writing clear to him.

14. This information is from oral tradition (Hemingway Birthplace Tour, Ernest Hemingway Foundation of Oak Park).

15. In *The Garden of Eden*, protagonist David Bourne writes his own Nick Adams–like story, a boyhood story of hunting in Africa with his father. The unpublished half of the *Eden* manuscript introduces yet another Nick, in this case a character who is central to the novel's second plot. (Neither this Nick nor this subplot appears in the published version.) Although this Nick is not named Adams, the name was simply too important to Hemingway for there not to be a deliberate resonance. See chapter 3.

16. In *The Garden of Eden,* Catherine experiments with becoming a "boy" and asks that David, likewise, try to be her "girl." David and Catherine do in bed what Hemingway did in the writing of "Hills."

17. Spilka ("Barbershop" 367), Smith (*Guide*), and Reynolds (*Chronology*) note the honeymoon composition of the story but do not address its possible critical ramifications.

18. The first and only holograph lists Hemingway's return address as "c/o Guaranty Trust" (KL/EH 473, 1), indicating that he was away from Paris. The absence of an emended typescript suggests professional preparation and that it was mailed to Perkins from the honeymoon, along with a letter dated May 27, 1927, stating, "Here are two more stories for the book [*Men Without Women*]" (*SL* 251).

19. Hemingway informed Perkins that "Stories like Fifty Grand, My Old Man and that sort are no where near as good stories, in the end, as a story like Hills Like White Elephants or Sea Change. But a book needs them because people understand them easily and it gives them the necessary confidence in the stories that are hard for them" (Bruccoli and Trogdon 188).

20. Parker characterizes "Hills" as "delicate and tragic" (94); Josephs implies that the story illustrates "the end of love" (58). Pamela Smiley's response differs in that she argues that both characters are simultaneously victims and perpetrators of "gender-linked miscommunication." She relocates responsibility for the "tragedy" but agrees with the majority that the outcome looks bleak.

21. Smith summarizes critical discussion of the various meanings of white elephant: "the realization of a mistake" (Sheldon Grebstein), "an annoyingly useless gift; . . . also . . . a possession of great value" (Joseph DeFalco), the unborn child and "a fully pregnant woman" (Lewis Weeks), and "a present" causing "ruin" (John Hollander) (*Guide* 208).

22. The extent to which the story's ending depends on which hills are like white elephants is evident from a mistranslation of "across" in the story's current French translation by Robillard and Duhamel, which begins "*A l'autre côté de la vallée*" (9). The story's title in this translation is, thus, "Paradis perdu [Paradise Lost]."

23. Collation reveals that the story was composed in three sittings: first draft, second sitting (revisions made on the same pages but at a later time), and final editing. The first draft appears to have been written rather quickly, in large, generously spaced letters, with very few same-draft changes. Second-sitting emendations are characterized by smaller handwriting, heavier pencil, and a different angle on the page, all of which are consistent throughout this set of emendations. No substantive material was added or deleted after this sitting.

24. Reynolds notes that Hemingway was in contact with Jinny, who had remained in Paris when her sister returned to Arkansas, and that Jinny "provided a shrewd analysis of what Pauline was facing in Piggott" (*Homecoming* 75). Information regarding Hemingway's feelings and actions during this period in what follows is drawn directly or inferred from his 1926 correspondence with Pauline (Baker and KL/EH Correspondence).

25. The line appears upside down, in between lines of the letter to Fitzgerald, which suggests that Hemingway typed the line and then reused the paper, explaining the line's strange appearance on the page to Fitzgerald, in the body of the letter, as "the start of something" (KL/EH Correspondence).

The Necessary Danger: Writing *The Garden of Eden*

1. In accordance with copyright law, quotations from *The Garden of Eden* in this chapter, although identified by their location within Hemingway's complete drafts of the novel, either (1) are present in the published text as well, (2) are cited as having been published in earlier criticism, or (3) in the rare instances where conditions (1) and (2) do not apply fall well within the guidelines of fair use under Title 17 of the U.S. Code in accordance with relevant case law concerning academic and scholarly criticism (for which current precedent is *Sundeman v. Seajay Society, Inc.*). Other unpublished matter is summarized in compliance with the guidelines of the Hemingway estate (Ernest Hemingway Foundation 153–57).

2. This chapter is based on draft(s) of this novel (KL/EH 422.1 and 422.2) rather than on Tom Jenks's 1986 edition, which invisibly elided three major characters and much of the story's structural complexity. The papers in 422.1 and 422.2 are comprised of intermingled, heavily emended manuscript and typescript pages. Because "draft" implies that there is a single draft contained in these files (there are probably two, dating from 1946 through 1958), and for ease, I use "the manuscript" and "the novel" as my default terms for the manuscript/typescript text(s)/draft(s) contained in these files.

3. See Burwell (xxiv–xxv) for a graphic representation of points of contiguity among Hemingway's postwar works.

4. The new country to which David refers is the sexual terrain he and Catherine are charting. However, a likely literary source for this metaphor—and, perhaps, his name—is Hamlet's "To be or not to be" soliloquy: "Who would fardels bear, / To grunt and sweat under a weary life, / But that the dread of something after death, / The undiscovered country from whose bourn / No traveler returns, puzzles the will, / And makes us rather bear those ills we have, / Than fly to others that we know not of? / Thus conscience does make cowards of us all" (3.1.77–84). "Bourn" refers to frontier or boundary (Bevington 1087), which David and Catherine are busy dissolving. Hemingway's copy of *Hamlet* was from his high school English class in 1916. The entry for *Hamlet* in Reynolds's *Hemingway's Reading* indicates that Hemingway had memorized Polonius's advice to Laertes and forty lines from III.ii (181).

5. The notion of direction without destination is the governing metaphor in *A Farewell to Arms* (see Justice).

6. "Remembering remembering" is the narrative device that governs "Now I Lay Me." See chapter 2.

7. Bruccoli locates Hemingway's first postmortem mention of Fitzgerald in his introduction to the 1948 edition of *A Farewell to Arms* and states that in 1949–50 alone, Hemingway wrote seven letters to Fitzgerald's main biographer, Arthur Mizener (*Friendship* 166).

8. For the connections between *The Great Gatsby* and *The Garden of Eden*, see Brogan, who argues that Harold Loeb's essay, "The Mysticism of Money," informs both *Gatsby* and *Eden.*

9. See, for example, Spilka ("Barbershop"), Comley, and Bruccoli (*Friendship*).

10. Spilka extends this argument but does not alter its basic premise in his 1990 study *Hemingway's Quarrel with Androgyny.*

11. See, for example, Burwell (66) and Eby (271).

12. Specifically in *A Farewell to Arms,* which I will discuss in the "Text" section of this chapter.

13. It is commonly acknowledged that this character is based on Edouard Jozan, the French naval flyer with whom Zelda was briefly besotted while the Fitzgeralds were guests of the Murphys on the Riviera. However, his status as a war hero (as Hemingway always depicted himself) and as a swaggering, good-natured man with an excellent tan also evokes the Hemingway from the same period.

14. Although this burning scene derives from two biographical sources (one of which had already appeared in his fiction, when Mrs. Adams burns Dr. Adams' collections in "Now I Lay Me" [KL/EH 618]; the other, Hadley Hemingway's loss of a valise of manuscripts in the early 1920s, appears three times in the postwar tetralogy: the burning scene in *The Garden of Eden;* as nonfiction in *A Moveable Feast;* and in "The Strange Country," originally part of the *Islands in the Stream* manuscript), by the writing of *Eden,* these incidents were ancient history. Hemingway had had twenty years to deal with the fact that Hadley had lost his manuscripts and twenty more to get used to the fact that his mother had burned his naturalist father's preserved specimens (including some rather Freudian snakes).

15. In *Tender Is the Night,* Fitzgerald also alludes to Ariel's song, referring to a group of Americans leaving Paris: "Standing in the station, with Paris in back of them, it seemed as if they were vicariously leaning a little over the ocean, already undergoing a sea-change, a shifting about of atoms to form the essential molecule of a new people" (83). Hemingway's story was published first; it is not clear whether Fitzgerald had read the story when he wrote this passage.

16. See, for example, Bruccoli and Baughman (59).

17. To illustrate how the synonymy breaks down between fertility and virility for Hemingway—and that the fact that it does is crucial—one need look no further than Jake Barnes in *The Sun Also Rises.* Barnes has testicles (and is thus technically fertile) but no penis (and is thus not virile).

18. See, for example, Eby (for discussion of *The Garden of Eden* alone, see 32, 167–68, 173, 208–12, 268, 325) and Fleming (*Face*), both of whom extensively elaborate on such moments and their importance to Hemingway's psyche and fiction.

19. Although it is tempting to attribute the focus on fertility to David's patriarchal conservatism, he does not cast the relationship in these terms—Catherine does, by projecting her fears about conservative gender roles onto David's sexual confusion and drawing her own conclusions. David is, if anything, a sexual submissive, becoming a girl at Catherine's request, kissing Marita at her request, and sleeping with Marita at her request. He draws the line at getting into bed with the two of them simultaneously.

20. Critics have long wondered if the wife in "Cat in the Rain" wants a baby (see Smith, *Guide* 46–48); several of Hemingway's biographers have cited Hadley Hemingway's pregnancy as a probable source for "Out of Season" (see Johnston 41–46; Meyers, *Biography* 154; Lynn 202).

21. Although Brasch and Sigman's catalog of Hemingway's library in Cuba lists *A Doll's House* as the only Ibsen play he owned, the similarities between *Hedda Gabler* and *The Garden of Eden* are striking. Indeed, the following description of Hedda and Thea maps exactly onto the characters of Catherine and Marita: "The central motive in the play is Hedda's desire to mold a human destiny. She conceives this destiny as a triumph

of the Dionysian spirit, for she would know vicariously an abandon that she cannot know in her own person; and she selects a man as her deputy because, having rejected her own womanhood, she identifies herself with the dominant male role . . . Hedda herself is high fashion. . . . The most exact foil to Hedda is the fragile young woman from the provinces [Thea] . . . who reveals little by little the fullness of womanly courage and passion" (Allison et al. 433).

A Pilgrim's Progress into Hell: *Death in the Afternoon* and the Problem of Authorship

1. This chapter is informed by an extension of Jerome McGann's social theory of textual transmission. In *A Critique of Modern Textual Criticism,* McGann argues that literary authority is a result of complex interactions among individuals, institutions, society, and culture. McGann's theory contests the romantic notion of authority, which holds that literary works are produced in isolation. He rejects the idea that an individual can "author" a work, identifying authorship not as a person but as a process, one in which the figure commonly identified as "the author" is but one node in a network of textual creation that includes editors, publishers, reviewers, etc. "Authority," McGann insists, "is a social nexus" (48). His insistence upon the intrinsically social quality of authorship and authority would have made sense to Ernest Hemingway. Hemingway's metacritical stance in *Death in the Afternoon* differs from McGann's argument in two ways. First, Hemingway draws a distinction between writer and author that McGann does not. (In this he anticipates by some sixty years Sean Burke's theoretical call for a situated embodied authorial subjectivity in discourses of authorship [ix].) Furthermore, Hemingway makes a judgment value that McGann does not espouse: that the contextual network required to bring a work of art to its public is intrinsically destructive to art and artist. For a more in-depth analysis of textual theories of authorship and the situation of this chapter within it, see the appendix.

2. Michel Foucault isolates the challenge of the author's name as a catalyst for incomprehension in discourses of authorship, noting that "the links between the proper name and the individual named and between the author's name and what it names are not isomorphic and do not function in the same way." Unlike a proper name, the author's name "performs a certain role with regard to narrative discourse, assuring a classificatory function" (227). *Death in the Afternoon* thus anticipates Foucault's work by several decades in that it implicitly asks and answers the question, "What is an author?"

3. Baker notes that the Old Lady was added relatively late in the writing of the book (214).

4. In *A Moveable Feast,* Hemingway responds to the phrase "mere sketch," using it scathingly, verbatim, from the perspective of a Nobel Prize–winning writer.

5. For this reason, his reference in excised portions of *The Garden of Eden* to Africa as having "no literature" did not imply, as one might expect, the racism of the exploitative white man expressing disdain for the illiterate natives but rather the appreciation of a man whose fame followed him everywhere. For Hemingway to have said that Africa had no "stories" would have been pejorative; by "no literature," he meant no publishing industry and thus none of the mechanisms of publicity—an absence he celebrated, not a lack he scorned. He valued his friendships with the fishermen in Cojímar, Cuba, for a

similar reason—because they did not speak English, had never read his books, and knew him personally and not through the media of print, they did not treat him like a famous author, although they knew he wrote books. To them, he was just the gringo who talked to them about fishing (*Sitios cubanos*).

6. Hemingway began working on *Death in the Afternoon* in March 1930 (Reynolds, *Chronology* 61).

Appendix: The Problem of Authorship and Textuality

1. West identifies copyright as the biggest challenge to textual scholars working with twentieth-century texts and discusses alternatives to editions.

2. Hemingway is not the only writer to evince such a fluid subjectivity; scholars have located similar fluidities in the cases of Twain (Lowry) and Yeats (Bornstein, "Remaking").

BIBLIOGRAPHY

Abbreviations

KL/EH—Items in the Hemingway Collection, John F. Kennedy Library, Boston. Numbers given in the text, e.g., 422.1/2, 15, indicate the file number (e.g., 422.1), folder number (e.g., 2), and page number (e.g., 15).

SL—Selected Letters of Ernest Hemingway (Ed. Carlos Baker)

Published Sources

Abdoo, Sherlyn. "Hemingway's 'Hills Like White Elephants.'" *Explicator* 49.4 (Summer 1991): 238–40.

Allison, Alexander W., Arthur J. Carr, and Arthur M. Eastman, eds. Introduction to *Hedda Gabler. Masterpieces of the Drama.* 5th ed. New York: Macmillan, 1986. 433–34.

Baker, Carlos. *Ernest Hemingway: A Life Story.* New York: Collier, 1969.

Barthes, Roland. "Authors and Writers." 1960. *A Barthes Reader.* Ed. Susan Sontag. New York: Hill and Wang, 1982. 185–93.

———. "The Death of the Author." 1968. *Image-Music-Text.* Trans. Stephen Heath. London: Fontana, 1977. 142–48.

Baudelaire, Charles. *The Flowers of Evil.* Ed. Marthiel and Jackson Matthews. Canada: Penguin Books, 1963.

Beach, Sylvia. *Shakespeare and Company: The Story of an American Bookshop in Paris.* New York: Harcourt Brace, 1956.

Benét's Reader's Encyclopedia. 3rd ed. New York: Harper Collins, 1987.

Benson, Jackson J. "Hemingway Criticism: Getting at the Hard Questions." *Hemingway: A Revaluation.* Ed. Donald R. Noble. Troy, N.Y.: Whitston, 1983. 7–47.

Bevington, David, ed. *The Complete Works of Shakespeare.* 3rd ed. London: Scott, Foresman, 1980.

Bornstein, George. "Introduction: Why Editing Matters." *Representing Modernist Texts: Editing as Interpretation.* Ed. George Bornstein. Ann Arbor: University of Michigan Press, 1991. 1–16.

———. "Remaking Himself: Yeats's Revisions of His Early Canon." *Text: Transactions of the Society for Textual Scholarship* 5 (1991): 339–58.

Bowers, Fredson. "Authorial Intention and Editorial Problems." *Text: Transactions of the Society for Textual Scholarship* 5 (1991): 49–61.

Boydston, Jo Ann. "Presidential Address, 1989: In Praise of Apparatus." *Text: Transactions of the Society for Textual Scholarship* 5 (1991): 1–13.

Brasch, James D., and Joseph Sigman. *Hemingway's Library: A Composite Record.* New York: Garland, 1981.

Breit, Harvey. "Success, It's Wonderful!" *New York Times Book Review* Dec. 3, 1950: 58. Bruccoli, *Conversations* 65.

———. "Talk with Mr. Hemingway." *New York Times Book Review* Sept. 17, 1950: 14. Bruccoli, *Conversations* 60–62.

Brogan, Jacqueline Vaught. "Strange Fruits in *The Garden of Eden:* 'The Mysticism of Money,' *The Great Gatsby*—and *A Moveable Feast.*" Kennedy and Bryer 235–56.

Bruccoli, Matthew J., ed. *Conversations with Ernest Hemingway.* Literary Conversations Series. Jackson: University of Mississippi Press, 1986.

———. *Fitzgerald and Hemingway: A Dangerous Friendship.* New York: Carroll & Graf, 1994.

———, with Judith S. Baughman. *Reader's Companion to F. Scott Fitzgerald's* Tender Is the Night. Columbia: University of South Carolina Press, 1996.

———, with Robert W. Trogdon, eds. *The Only Thing That Counts: The Ernest Hemingway–Maxwell Perkins Correspondence.* New York: Scribner's, 1996.

Bryer, Jackson R., and Cathy W. Barks, eds. *Dear Scott, Dearest Zelda: The Love Letters of F. Scott and Zelda Fitzgerald.* New York: St. Martin's Press, 2002.

Bunyan, John. *Pilgrim's Progress.* 1678. *The Norton Anthology of English Literature.* Ed. M. H. Abrams. Vol. 1. 5th ed. New York: W. W. Norton, 1986. 1863–72.

Burke, Sean. *The Death and Return of the Author: Criticism and Subjectivity in Barthes, Foucault and Derrida.* 2nd ed. Edinburgh: Edinburgh University Press, 1998.

Burwell, Rose Marie. *Hemingway: The Postwar Years and the Posthumous Novels.* Cambridge Studies in American Literature and Culture, 96. Cambridge: Cambridge University Press, 1996.

Coates, Robert M. "Bullfighters." *New Yorker* Oct. 1, 1932: 61–63. Meyers, *Critical Heritage* 160–62.

Collins, Angus. "F. Scott Fitzgerald: Homosexuality and the Genesis of *Tender Is the Night.*" *Journal of Modern Literature* 13 (March 1986): 167–71.

Comley, Nancy R. "Madwomen on the Riviera: The Fitzgeralds, Hemingway, and the Matter of Modernism." Kennedy and Bryer 277–96.

———, and Robert Scholes. *Hemingway's Genders: Rereading the Hemingway Text.* New Haven, Conn.: Yale University Press, 1994.

Copyright Term Extension Act. Pub. L. 105–289. Oct. 27, 1998. Stat. 2827.

Cowley, Malcolm. "A Farewell to Spain." *New Republic* Nov. 30, 1932: 76–77. Meyers, *Critical Heritage* 164–69.

Dante Alighieri. *The Inferno. The Divine Comedy.* Trans. Henry Wadsworth Longfellow. Garden City: Doubleday & Co. nd.

———. *Inferno. The Divine Comedy.* Trans. Robert Pinsky. New York: Farrar, Straus and Giroux, 1994.

——— *La divina commedia.* Trans. Lawrence Binyon. *World Masterpieces.* Ed. Maynard Mack et al. Vol. 1. New York: W. W. Norton, 1965. 851–1022.

Darnton, Robert. "What Is the History of Books?" *Reading in America: Literature and Social History.* Ed. Cathy N. Davidson. Baltimore: Johns Hopkins University Press, 1989. 27–52.

Donaldson, Scott. *Hemingway vs. Fitzgerald: The Rise and Fall of a Literary Friendship.* Woodstock, N.Y.: Overlook Press, 1999.

———. "Preparing for the End: Hemingway's Revisions of 'A Canary for One.'" *Studies in American Fiction* 6 (Autumn 1978): 203–11.

Duffus, R. L. "Hemingway Now Writes of Bull-Fighting as an Art." *New York Times Book Review* 25 September 1932: 5+. Stephens 112–13.

Eby, Carl P. *Hemingway's Fetishism: Psychoanalysis and the Mirror of Manhood.* Albany: State University of New York Press, 1999.

Eliade, Mircea. *Le sacré et le profane.* Paris: Gallimard, 1987.

Ernest Hemingway Foundation. "Procedures for Requesting Permission to Publish Portions of the Works of Ernest Hemingway." *Hemingway Review* 16.2 (Spring 1997): 153–57.

Fitch, Noel Riley. *Sylvia Beach and the Lost Generation: A History of Literary Paris in the Twenties and Thirties.* New York: W. W. Norton, 1983.

Fitzgerald, F. Scott. *Tender Is the Night.* 1933. New York: Scribner's, 1995.

———. *This Side of Paradise.* New York: Scribner's, 1920.

Fleming, Robert E. *The Face in the Mirror: Hemingway's Writers.* Tuscaloosa: University of Alabama Press, 1994.

———. "Perversion and the Writer in 'The Sea Change.'" *Studies in American Fiction* 14 (1986): 215–20.

Foucault, Michel. "What Is an Author?" 1969. *The Book History Reader.* Ed. David Finkelstein and Alistair McCleery. London: Routledge, 2002. 225–30.

Friedan, Betty. *The Feminine Mystique.* 1962–1963. New York: Dell, 1983.

Greetham, D. C., ed. *Scholarly Editing: A Guide to Research.* New York: Modern Language Association of America, 1995.

Hagopian, John V. "Symmetry in 'Cat in the Rain.'" *College English* 24 (Dec. 1962): 220–22.

Hanneman, Audre. *Ernest Hemingway: A Comprehensive Bibliography.* Princeton, N.J.: Princeton University Press, 1967.

Hannum, Howard L. "'Jig Jig to Dirty Ears': White Elephants to Let." *Hemingway Review* 11.1 (Spring 1991): 46–59.

Hemingway, Ernest. *Across the River and Into the Trees.* New York: Scribner's, 1950.

———. "Big Two-Hearted River I." 1925. Hemingway, *Complete Short Stories* 163–69.

———. "Big Two-Hearted River II." 1925. Hemingway, *Complete Short Stories* 173–80.

———. "A Canary for One." 1927. Hemingway, *Complete Short Stories* 258–61.

———. "A Canary for One." Drafts. Files 307, 308, 309. Hemingway Collection. John F. Kennedy Library, Boston.

———. "Cat in the Rain." 1925. Hemingway, *Complete Short Stories* 129–31.

———. "Cat in the Rain." Drafts. Files 319, 320, 321, 322, 323, 670.1. Hemingway Collection. John F. Kennedy Library, Boston.

———. *The Complete Short Stories of Ernest Hemingway.* Finca Vigia Edition. New York: Scribner's, 1987.

———. Correspondence. Hemingway Collection. John F. Kennedy Library, Boston.

———. "Cross-Country Snow." 1925. Hemingway, *Complete Short Stories* 143–47.

———. "Cross-Country Snow." Drafts. Files 344, 345, 346, 696. Hemingway Collection. John F. Kennedy Library, Boston.

———. *Death in the Afternoon.* New York: Scribner's, 1932.

———. *Death in the Afternoon.* Galley proofs. Cohn Hemingway Collection. University of Delaware. Newark, Del.

———. "The Doctor and the Doctor's Wife." 1925. Hemingway, *Complete Short Stories* 73–76.

———. "The Doctor and the Doctor's Wife." Drafts. Files 202c, 728, 729. Hemingway Collection. John F. Kennedy Library, Boston.

———. "The End of Something." 1924. Hemingway, *Complete Short Stories* 79–82.

———. *A Farewell to Arms.* New York: Scribner's, 1929.

———. "Fathers and Sons." Hemingway, *Complete Short Stories* 369–77.

———. *The Fifth Column and Four Unpublished Stories of the Spanish Civil War.* New York: Scribner's, 1969.

———. *For Whom the Bell Tolls.* New York: Scribner's, 1940.

———. *The Garden of Eden.* New York: Scribner's, 1986.

———. *The Garden of Eden.* Drafts. Files 422.1, 422.2, 422.9. Hemingway Collection. John F. Kennedy Library, Boston.

———. *Green Hills of Africa.* New York: Scribner's, 1935.

———. "Hills Like White Elephants." 1927. Hemingway, *Complete Short Stories* 211–14.

———. "Hills Like White Elephants." Drafts. Files 472, 473. Hemingway Collection. John F. Kennedy Library, Boston.

———. "In Another Country." 1927. Hemingway, *Complete Short Stories* 206–10.

———. "In Another Country." Drafts. Files 492, 492a, 507. Hemingway Collection. John F. Kennedy Library, Boston.

———. *In Our Time.* New York: Boni & Liveright, 1925.

———. *In Our Time.* 2nd ed. New York: Boni & Liveright, 1930.

———. *In Our Time.* Paris: Three Mountains Press, 1924.

———. *Islands in the Stream.* New York: Scribner's, 1970.

———. "The Last Good Country." 1972. Hemingway, *Complete Short Stories* 504–44.

———. List. File 422.9 Hemingway Collection. John F. Kennedy Library, Boston.

———. List of Stories to Write. File 720a. Hemingway Collection. John F. Kennedy Library, Boston.

———. *Men Without Women.* New York: Scribner's, 1927.

———. *A Moveable Feast.* New York: Scribner's, 1964.

———. *The Nick Adams Stories.* New York: Scribner's, 1972.

———. "Nobel Prize Acceptance Speech." Bruccoli, *Conversations* 196–98.

———. "Now I Lay Me." 1927. Hemingway, *Complete Short Stories* 276–82.

———. "Now I Lay Me." Drafts. Files 618, 619, 620, 622. Hemingway Collection. John F. Kennedy Library, Boston.

———. "Now I Lay Me." Hemingway, *Men Without Women* 218–32.

———. *The Old Man and the Sea.* New York: Scribner's, 1952.

———. "The Old Man at the Bridge." 1938. Hemingway, *Complete Short Stories* 57–58.

———. "Out of Season." 1925. Hemingway, *Short Stories* 173–79.

———. "Out of Season." Draft. File 644. Hemingway Collection. John F. Kennedy Library, Boston.

———. *Paradis perdu suivi de la cinquième colonne.* 1949. Trans. Henri Robillard and Marcel Duhamel. France: Gallimard/Folio, 1995.

———. "The Sea Change." 1933. Hemingway, *Complete Short Stories* 302–5.

———. "The Sea Change." Drafts. Files 222, 678, 679, 680, 681, 681a, 734, 735. Hemingway Collection. John F. Kennedy Library, Boston.

———. *Selected Letters 1917–1961.* Ed. Carlos Baker. New York: Charles Scribner's Sons, 1981.

———. "The Short Happy Life of Francis Macomber." 1938. Hemingway, *Complete Short Stories* 5–28.

———. "The Short Happy Life of Francis Macomber." Drafts. Files 689, 690, 691, 692. Hemingway Collection. John F. Kennedy Library, Boston.

———. *Short Stories of Ernest Hemingway.* New York: Scribner's. 1938.

———. "The Snows of Kilimanjaro." 1938. Hemingway, *Complete Short Stories* 39–56.

———. "The Snows of Kilimanjaro." Drafts. Files 702, 703, 704, 705, 706. Hemingway Collection. John F. Kennedy Library, Boston.

———. *The Sun Also Rises.* New York: Scribner's, 1926.

———. "Ten Indians." 1927. Hemingway, *Complete Short Stories* 253–57.

———. "Ten Indians." Drafts. Files 202C, 727, 728, 729, 730. Hemingway Collection. John F. Kennedy Library, Boston.

———. "The Three-Day Blow." 1924. Hemingway, *Complete Short Stories* 85–93.

———. *Three Stories and Ten Poems.* Paris: Contact, 1923.

———. *To Have and Have Not.* New York: Scribner's, 1937.

———. *The Torrents of Spring.* New York: Scribner's, 1926.

———. *True at First Light.* New York: Scribner's, 1999.

———. *True at First Light.* Drafts. Files 223a, 223b. Hemingway Collection. John F. Kennedy Library. Boston.

———. "Up in Michigan." 1921–1922. Hemingway, *Short Stories* 81–86.

———. *Winner Take Nothing.* New York: Scribner's, 1933.

Hemingway, Patrick. "An Evening with Patrick Hemingway." *Hemingway Review* 19.1 (Fall 1999): 8–16.

Hicks, Granville. "Bulls and Bottles." *Nation* Nov. 9, 1932: 461. Meyers, *Critical Heritage* 162–64.

Hotchner, A. E. *Papa Hemingway: A Personal Memoir.* New York: Carroll & Graf, 1999.

Ibsen, Henrik. *Hedda Gabler. Masterpieces of the Drama.* Ed. Alexander W. Allison, Arthur J. Carr, and Arthur M. Eastman. 433–78.

"Jig." *Webster's Revised Unabridged Dictionary.* Ed. Noah Porter. New York: G. & C. Merriam Co., 1913. 800.

Johnston, Kenneth G. "Hemingway's 'Out of Season' and the Psychology of Errors." *Literature and Psychology* 21 (Nov. 1971): 41–46.

Josephs, Allen. "How Did Hemingway Write?" *North Dakota Quarterly* 63.3 (Summer 1996): 50–64.

Junkins, Donald. "The Poetry of the Twentieth Chapter of *Death in the Afternoon:* Relationships between the Deleted and Published Halves." *Hemingway in Italy and Other Essays.* Ed. Robert W. Lewis. New York: Praeger, 1990. 113–21.

Justice, Hilary K. "Alias Grace: Music and the Feminine Aesthetic in Hemingway's Early Style." *Hemingway and Women: Female Critics and the Female Voice in Hemingway.*

Ed. Lawrence Broer and Gloria Holland. Tuscaloosa: University of Alabama Press, 2002. 221–38.

Kennedy, J. Gerald. *Imagining Paris: Exile, Writing, and American Identity.* New Haven, Conn.: Yale University Press, 1993.

———, and Jackson R. Bryer, eds. *French Connections: Hemingway and Fitzgerald Abroad.* New York: St. Martin's, 1998.

Kert, Bernice. *The Hemingway Women.* New York: W. W. Norton, 1998.

Kozikowski, Stanley. "Hemingway's 'Hills Like White Elephants.'" *Explicator* 52 (Winter 1994): 107–9.

Leach, Henry Goddard. Letter to Ernest Hemingway. June 28, 1929. Hemingway Collection, John F. Kennedy Library, Boston.

———. Letter to Ernest Hemingway. May 2, 1930. Hemingway Collection, John F. Kennedy Library, Boston.

Los sitios cubanos de Ernest Hemingway. Videocassette. Cuba: n.d.

Lowry, Richard S. *"Littery Man": Mark Twain and Modern Authorship.* Commonwealth Center Studies in American Culture. Oxford: Oxford University Press, 1996.

Lynn, Kenneth S. *Hemingway.* New York: Fawcett Columbine, 1987.

Mandel, Miriam B. *Reading Hemingway: The Facts in the Fictions.* Metuchen, N.J.: Scarecrow Press, 1995.

McGann, Jerome J. *A Critique of Modern Textual Criticism.* 1983. Charlottesville: University of Virginia Press, 1992.

———. "A Response to T. H. Howard-Hill." *Text: Transactions of the Society for Textual Scholarship* 5 (1991): 47–48.

———. "What Is Critical Editing?" *Text: Transactions of the Society for Textual Scholarship* 5 (1991): 15–29.

Mencken, H. L. "The Spanish Idea of a Good Time." *American Mercury* Dec. 1932: 506–07. Meyers, *Critical Heritage* 170–72.

Meyers, Jeffrey, ed. *Ernest Hemingway: The Critical Heritage.* Critical Heritage Series. London: Routledge, 1982.

———. *Hemingway: A Biography.* New York: Harper, 1985.

Milford, Nancy. *Zelda: A Biography.* New York: Harper & Row, 1970.

Moddelmog, Debra A. *Reading Desire: In Pursuit of Ernest Hemingway.* Ithaca, N.Y.: Cornell University Press, 1999.

Nakjavani, Erik. "The Aesthetics of Silence: Hemingway's Art of the Short Story." *Hemingway Review* 3.2 (Spring 1984): 38–45.

Nehamas, Alexander. "Writer, Text, Work, Author." *Literature and the Question of Philosophy.* Ed. Anthony J. Cascardi. Baltimore: Johns Hopkins University Press, 1987. 267–91.

O'Brien, Timothy D. "Allusion, Word-Play, and the Central Conflict in 'Hills Like White Elephants.'" *Hemingway Review* 12.1 (Fall 1992): 19–26.

Parker, Dorothy. "Review of *Men Without Women.*" *New Yorker* Oct. 29, 1927: 92–94.

Patterson, Curtis. "The Ancients Are Ancients—." *Town & Country* Oct. 15, 1932: 50. Stephens 118–19.

Proust, Marcel. *The Remembrance of Things Past.* Trans. C. K. Scott Moncrieff and Terence Kilmartin. Vol. 1. New York: Vintage, 1981.

Raeburn, John. *Fame Became of Him: Hemingway as Public Writer.* Bloomington: Indiana University Press, 1984.

Renner, Stanley. "Moving to the Girl's Side of 'Hills Like White Elephants.'" *Hemingway Review* 15.1 (Fall 1995): 27–41.

Renza, Louis A. "The Importance of Being Ernest." 1989. Wagner-Martin 213–38.

Reynolds, Michael S. *Hemingway: An Annotated Chronology.* Detroit, Mich.: Omnigraphics, 1991.

———. *Hemingway: The American Homecoming.* Oxford: Basil Blackwell, 1992.

———. *Hemingway: The Final Years.* New York: W. W. Norton, 1999.

———. *Hemingway: The Paris Years.* Oxford: Basil Blackwell, 1989.

———. *Hemingway in the 1930s.* New York: W. W. Norton, 1997.

———. *Hemingway's Reading, 1910–1940: An Inventory.* Princeton, N.J.: Princeton University Press, 1981.

———. *The Young Hemingway.* Oxford: Basil Blackwell, 1986.

Sandison, David. *Ernest Hemingway: An Illustrated Biography.* Chicago: Chicago Review Press, 1998.

Shakespeare, William. *Hamlet.* Bevington 1069–1120.

———. *Romeo and Juliet.* Bevington 994–1031.

———. *The Tempest.* Bevington 1497–525.

Smiley, Pamela. "Gender-Linked Miscommunication in 'Hills Like White Elephants.'" *Hemingway Review* 8.1 (Fall 1988): 2–12.

Smith, Paul. "Hemingway's Short Fiction Through the Manuscripts." Lecture to Graduate Seminar. Ed. Paul Smith. Trinity College, Hartford, Conn. 1994.

———. "Introduction: Hemingway and the Practical Reader." *New Essays on Hemingway's Short Fiction.* Ed. Paul Smith. The American Novel. Cambridge: Cambridge University Press, 1998. 1–18.

———. *A Reader's Guide to the Short Stories of Ernest Hemingway.* Boston: McGraw Hill, 1989.

Spilka, Mark. "Hemingway's Barbershop Quintet: *The Garden of Eden* Manuscript." Wagner-Martin 349–72.

———. *Hemingway's Quarrel with Androgyny.* Lincoln: University of Nebraska Press, 1990.

Stein, Gertrude. *The Autobiography of Alice B. Toklas.* New York: Harcourt Brace, 1933.

Stephens, Robert O., ed. *Ernest Hemingway: The Critical Reception.* The American Critical Tradition. N.p.: Burt Franklin & Co., 1977.

Sundeman v. Seajay Society, Inc. 142 F.3d 194. 4th Cir. 1998.

Tanselle, G. Thomas. *A Rationale of Textual Criticism.* Philadelphia: University of Pennsylvania Press, 1989.

———. "The Varieties of Scholarly Editing." Greetham 9–32.

Tolkien, J. R. R. Foreword to the Second Edition. *The Fellowship of the Ring.* Boston: Houghton Mifflin, 1965. 5–8.

Trilling, Lionel. "Review of *The Fifth Column and the First Forty-Nine Stories.*" *Partisan Review* 6 (Winter 1939): 52–60. Meyers, *Critical Heritage* 278–88.

Trogdon, Robert W. "Hemingway and Scribners: The Professional Relationship." Ph.D. diss. University of South Carolina, 1996.

Vaill, Amanda. *Everybody Was So Young: Gerald and Sara Murphy—A Lost Generation Love Story.* Boston: Houghton Mifflin, 1998.

Wagner-Martin, Linda, ed. *Hemingway: Seven Decades of Criticism.* East Lansing: Michigan State University Press, 1998.

West, James L. W., III. "Twentieth-Century American and British Literature." Greetham 365–81.

White, Gertrude M. "We're All 'Cats in the Rain.'" *Fitzgerald-Hemingway Annual* (1978): 241–46.

INDEX

skiing, 26. *See also* motifs

Smiley, Pamela, 44, 138n11, 141n20

Smith, D. J., and Mrs. ("Up in Michigan"), 76, 124–26

Smith, Paul, 3, 20, 22, 27, 29, 37, 40, 43–44, 49, 52–53, 72–73, 96, 124, 126–27, 137n1, 138n5, 141nn17, 20, 143n20

"The Snows of Kilimanjaro." *See under* Hemingway, Ernest, works of

Spain, 58, 88–89, 111. *See also* Barcelona; Madrid; Pamplona

Spilka, Mark, 6, 10, 18–19, 63–65, 72, 88, 90, 137n3, 141n18, 142nn9, 10

Stein, Gertrude, 15, 20, 28, 66, 140n6; *The Autobiography of Alice B. Toklas,* 66

suitcases, 21, 29, 37, 40, 42, 47, 52–53, 70–72, 85, 121, 127. *See also* motifs

The Sun Also Rises. See under Hemingway, Ernest, works of

Switzerland, 29, 32–33, 123, 140n8. *See also* Vevey

Taming of the Shrew. See under Shakespeare, William, works of

Tanselle, G. Thomas, 130

The Tempest. See under Shakespeare, William, works of

"Ten Indians." *See under* Hemingway, Ernest, works of

textual autobiography, 58, 121. *See also* Hemingway, Ernest, genre

textual theory, 14, 129–36, 145n1

This Side of Paradise. See under Fitzgerald, F. Scott

"The Three-Day Blow." *See under* Hemingway, Ernest, works of

Three Stories and Ten Poems. See under Hemingway, Ernest, works of

Tiny ("Out of Season"), 124–25

To Have and Have Not. See under Hemingway, Ernest, works of Tolkien, J. R. R. 1, 2

Toronto, Ontario, 21

The Torrents of Spring. See under Hemingway, Ernest, works of

"The Tradesman Returns." *See under* Hemingway, Ernest, works of

tragedy, 104, 141n20. *See also* Hemingway, Ernest, genre

Trilling, Lionel, 68, 137n2

Trogdon, Robert W., 62, 68. *See also* Bruccoli, Matthew J.: with

True at First Light. See under Hemingway, Ernest, works of

Twain, Mark, 145n2

Ulysses. See under Joyce, James, work of

Under Kilimanjaro. See under Hemingway, Ernest, works of

United States of America, 15–16, 26, 35, 52–53, 62, 89, 123, 128. *See also* Chicago, Illinois; Horton's Bay, Michigan; Key West, Florida; Michigan; Oak Park, Illinois; Piggott, Arkansas

"Up in Michigan." *See under* Hemingway, Ernest, works of

Ur-Text, 19, 127. *See also* Hemingway, Ernest, genre

Vaill, Amanda, 140n6

Vevey, Switzerland, 29, 32–33

virility tales, 6, 8, 13, 14, 16, 16t, 17t, 18–19, 20t, 21–22, 23–29, 55, 56t, 58, 74, 123–24, 127, 138n6, 140n15. *See also* Hemingway, Ernest, genre

"Vive le cast iron seal. . . ." *See under* Pinkham, Lydia

vocation/occupation, 4, 10, 55, 56t, 64, 68, 87, 90. *See also* finances

Vogue (magazine), 34

Welsh, Mary, 2, 9, 28, 61

West, James L., III, 131–32, 145n1

"What Is an Author?" 129

White, Gertrude M., 22

the wife: in "A Canary for One," 29, 32–34; in "Cat in the Rain," 22–23, 143n20

wilderness 26, 114. *See also* motifs

Wilson, Edmund, 68

Winner Take Nothing. See under Hemingway, Ernest, works of

The Winter's Tale. See under Shakespeare, William, works of

World War II, 13, 58, 61

writer/author, 4–5, 9, 14, 34–36, 56t, 60, 69, 74, 80, 82–87, 129–36, 140n13, 144n1, 144–45n5, 145n2

Yeats, William Butler, 145n2